प्रत्यभिज्ञाहृदयम्

Pratyabhijñāhṛdayam

of *Kṣemarāja*

The Essence of Self-Recognition

Interpretation and practical notes by Dmitri Semenov

January 2003 –January 2008

Sattarka Publications

ISBN 978-0-615-26268-0

Library of Congress Control Number: 2008911179

Cover photograph provided courtesy of Lance Wiskowski ©
(shot at Phnom Rung, May 2003) `ultraluminousgraphic.com`

To Swami Shambhavananda,
whose casual remark turned
my attention to the excellent
Pratyabhijñāhṛdayam

To Alexander Orekhov,
who taught me modern
psychology.

To my wife Elena
and son Andrei,
for their patience
and understanding.

Contents

Preface **vii**
On reading books . . . vii
Scriptural sources . . . viii
Acknowledgments . . . ix

Introduction **1**
Scope . . . 1
Problem . . . 1
Methods . . . 2
Attitudes . . . 5

Sanskrit Text **8**

Concepts **9**
aṇu . . . 18
vikalpa . . . 21
śiva and *śakti* . . . 29
Shakti . . . 30
Tattvas . . . 32
Malas . . . 46
Meditation . . . 49

Postulates **53**
Sutra 1 . . . 54
Sutra 2 . . . 56
Sutra 3 . . . 57
Sutra 4 . . . 59
Sutra 5 . . . 63
Sutra 6 . . . 64
Sutra 7 . . . 68
Sutra 8 . . . 70

Sutra 9 75
Sutra 10 76
Sutra 11 78
Sutra 12 79
Sutra 13 80
Sutra 14 81
Sutra 15 82
Sutra 16 83
Sutra 17 84
Sutra 18 85
Sutra 19 87
Sutra 20 88

Appendix A **89**

Appendix B **96**

Appendix C **99**

Bibliography **101**

Index **102**

Preface

What is presented here is not an academic work, but rather organized and referenced personal notes made in the pursuit of enlightenment. They touch upon a single facet of a complex and multidimensional philosophical system called *Pratyabhijñā*, or the system of recognition of the pure form of Self. The current exposition is based on a particular elucidation of the system — that of *Pratyabhijñāhṛdayam* by Kshemaraja.

Pratyabhijñā was originally formulated in the context of a larger system called Trika, which belongs to the tradition of Kashmir Shaivism. Therefore, it shares many concepts with other Indian philosophies of liberation, in particular, with Patanjali Yoga, Vedanta, and Buddhism.

Pratyabhijñā was developed in a text called *Śivadṛṣṭi*, composed by the sage Somananda; Utpaladeva elaborated on it in *Īśvarapratyabhijñākārikā*; it was simplified and condensed by Kshemaraja in *Pratyabhijñāhṛdayam* and extensively commented upon by Abhinavagupta.

On reading books

There is no book that gives a recipe for enlightenment, and no sage has the power to impart it, for the certainty of knowing shines only within. On a spiritual path "direct experience alone has access to the source of real knowledge."[1]

It is not possible to replicate the path of another, for one's own path will be as unique as the iris of one's eye.

Notwithstanding this uniqueness, if one approaches the problem with the resolve to discover and to experiment, then the vast body of scriptural knowledge and the spirit of living traditions will be of greatest help.

[1] See "Direct Experience Alone is the Means" in [Ram99].

Here is a list of books that I found to be helpful with understanding specifics of the *Pratyabhijñā*, in no particular order:

Īśvarapratyabhijñākārikā of Utpaladeva with the Authors's V.rtti, by Raffaele Torella, Motilal Banarsidass, 2002

Pratyabhijñāhṛdayam, The Secret of Self-Recognition, by Jaideva Singh, Motilal Banarsidass, 2003

Kashmir Shaivism, The Secret Supreme, by Swami Lakshmanjoo, Kashmir Shaivism Fellowship, 2000

Nothing Exists That is not Shiva, by Swami Muktananda, SYDA Foundation, 1997

The Splendor of Recognition, by Swami Shantananda, SYDA Foundation, 2003

Scriptural sources

Here are scriptural sources used and abbreviations for them.

TA	*Tantrāloka* by Abhinavagupta
AbhTs	*Tantrasāra* by Abhinavagupta
IPK	*Īśvarapratyabhijñākārikā* by Utpaladeva
ShS	*Śivasūtra*
ShSv	*Śivasvarodaya*
VBh	*Vijñānabhairava*
BhG	*Bhagavadgītā*
YS	*Yogasūtra* by Patanjali
SvaT	*Svacchandatantra*
MrA	*Mṛgendrāgama*
TtP	*Tattvaprakāśa*
HYP	*Haṭhayogapradīpika* by Svatmarama
ShSVR	*Śivasūtravārtika*
ManUp	*Māṇḍukyopaniṣad*

ShV *Śāktavijñāna* by Somananda

AN Anguttara Nikaya, Sutta Pitaka

SN Samyutta Nikaya, Sutta Pitaka

DN Digha Nikaya

DhP Dhammapada

Acknowledgments

I am very grateful to Alexey Tuzhilin, extensive discussions with whom helped to shape this book, and who inspired me to continue writing it. Special thanks to Shae Isaacs who undertook the hard work of editing the draft of the book and to Lance Wiskowski who graciously gave permission to use his photograph for the front cover.

The biggest source of amazement while practicing *Pratyabhijñā* philosophy was the ever expanding horizons of the plasticity of psyche, but I have tried to keep the ratio of mystical exaltation over practicality in here as small as possible. My hope is that this book will lessen the frustration of translating the very obscure language of traditional written sources into practical methods, at least for people with background in hard sciences.

Introduction

Scope

If one were to use two distinct categories of things, "the mental" and "the physical," then "the mental" is the only subject of this philosophical investigation. Practically, it is helpful to imagine the receptive fields of our sense organs: the retina, the cochlea, the skin, the taste buds of the tounge, the olfactory bulbs of the nose, etc., and to contemplate the fact that what is given to us as the perceived Universe is only a stream of stimulation on the surface of those receptive fields. The rest — three dimensional space, time, colors, music, faces, objects, landscapes, etc. — is an interpretation of those streams of stimulation by our psychic systems. *Pratyabhijñā* concerns itself mostly with what happens during such interpretation, not with the physical structure of the Universe. Therefore, in what follows the term "Universe" means "the entire Universe as reflected in one's own being."

Problem

A universal philosophical proposition is that "the senses deceive the mind."[2] The appearance of things given in sensations, and the mental ideas, formed of them, are, unless one follows carefully designed method, indeterminate, variable, unstable, illusory and subject to errors.[3]

There are at least two ways to make the deception less pervasive. One is to arm the mind and the senses with tools that make perception and reasoning more robust, self-correcting, and universal.

[2] As Diogenes Laertius put it, "The senses are deceivers, and reason disagrees with itself."

[3] For extensive discussion, see Bertrand Russell, *Problems of Philosophy: Appearance and Reality.*

The other one is to purify perception and reasoning from factors that facilitate the deception, like desires, emotions, and concepts of "self."

Whereas Western philosophical traditions, pursuing the first path, design tools like logic, mathematics, Socratic method of hypothesis, etc., and scientific instruments that enhance our senses, Indian doctrines of liberation pursue the second path, aiming to remove the emotional, ego-related, and psycho-physiological sources of the deception. If natural philosophy is to bring into the sphere of to-be-known as yet unknown aspects of the physical world, then yoga is to make knowable the hidden inner realms.

It should be noted that the ability to use logic or to follow the Socratic method of hypothesis or the Cartesian method of systematic doubt presupposes at least a partial independence of processes of perception, cognition, and reasoning from the emotional plane of psyche, from all personal constructs, from ego, etc. Though this independence occurs naturally, without any special training, it is sporadic and vulnerable to pressures of necessity and time constraints. The doctrines of liberation aim at attaining robust[4] independence in a systematic fashion. When this independence is universal, pervasive, and permanent, it is called "enlightenment."

"Enlightenment is a state of freedom from the ignorance that causes suffering..."[5][Ram82].

Methods

Any systematic practice, derived from a doctrine of liberation, is called *yoga*.[6] A set of such practices, individualized and adjusted to circumstances, is called *sādhana*.

Practices of the *Pratyabhijñā* system are of three types: analytical, practices of concentration, and psycho-physiological. Analytical practices consist of finding out the configuration of certain psychological processes and reconfiguring them. Concentration practices are those of focused concentration, meditation, and *samādhi*. Psycho-physiological practices are those that work with

[4]Robustness is of essense, for if the subtlety of one's state is ruined by a morsel of food or a smile from a nice girl, it is not much of an achievement. Methods relying on emaciation or starvation of the powers of the mind or of the body, lead primarily to non-robust results. That is why Buddha abandoned such methods.

[5]More technical definition will be given later, when necessary concepts are defined.

[6]The Bhagavad Gita gives a good idea of the variety of *yoga*-s.

posture (*āsana*), breath and flows of vital energies such as *prāṇa*, *apāna*, etc. (see [Dev87] for extensive treatment of these pratices).

Results of the practices are determined in part by the philosophical position one adopts. For example, if one practices *āsana*-s, while adopting materialistic position, then benefits would be limited primarily to stretching, exercising muscles, and massage of glands. If, on the other hand, one practices the same *āsana*-s but adopts the philosophy of hatha yoga, then, in addition to the benefits mentioned, one would develop dispassion toward one's physical body and gain higher level of awareness.

Another example is provided by the ethics of relations. If one adopts the position that an ethical treatment of others is nothing more than an internalized threat of punishment by authorities, then following ethical rules would create a growing sense of rebellion. If, on the contrary, one follows the same rules but adopts the principle of non-violence (*ahiṃsā*) towards sentient beings, then among the results would be a sense of tranquility and sympathetic friendliness.

One reason for this dependence of practice results on an adopted philosophical position is that many practices bring perception, cognition, emotions, and somatic processes into a state that is indeterminate and unstable to a much higher degree than what occurs naturally. An adopted philosophical position, whether it is adopted consciously, subconsciously, or unconsciously, influences how this indeterminacy will be resolved. Philosophical systems conducive to the pursuit of enlightenment promote psychological plasticity, avoidance of opinions where they can be avoided, and moderation in all aspects of life.

Another reason for the dependence of practice results on an adopted philosophical position is the fact that the ideas one has about the object of investigation (that is, one's own mental phenomena) might change that very object.

To address this dependence, there are two threads of exposition: one provides an analytical framework that affords relative stability of the object of the investigation; the other outlines procedures for an effective transformation of the same.

Thus, for the approach, adopted here, a study of the conceptual system and of major postulates is of the essence.

There are two major classes of procedural content for any system of liberation. One group is called *sattarka*, or *true reasoning.* The other is called *bhakti*, or *wholesome devotion to a deity or to a guru.*

The procedural content of the *Pratyabhijñā* system belongs primarily to the methods of *sattarka*. As said in the *Pūrvaśāstra*, reasoning is the highest component of *yoga*.[7] The choice between the *sattarka* and the *bhakti* paths, or a choice of balance between the two, is to be made in accordance with individual disposition. The path of *bhakti* will not be touched upon in this book.

An important component of a *sattarka* path is pragmatic empiricism, as expounded in the Kalama Sutta (AN.3.65):

> Do not go upon what is heard frequently;
> nor upon a tradition;
> nor upon a rumor;
> nor upon a scripture;
> nor upon a conjecture;
> nor upon an inference;
> nor upon an analogy;
> nor upon compatibility with various views;
> nor upon another's seeming ability;
> nor upon the consideration, "This contemplative is our teacher."
>
> ...when you yourselves know: "*These* things are favorable; *these* things are not injurious; *these* things are praised by the wise; *these* things, undertaken and observed, lead to benefit and happiness," adopt them and abide in them.

One might take tradition, scriptures, teachings imparted by a teacher, etc., very seriously, but one should not take knowledge gained from these sources as a manifest truth, for such truth is obtained only through one's own direct experience. Tradition, scriptures, teachers, the example set by an advanced practitioner, inferences, etc., might be excellent guides that lead away from errors, but one's own experience is the only ever-present light.

There is nothing supernatural about the process of attaining enlightenment or about the result; it is not necessary to have belief in God [Ram82]. Everyone has an inborn potential for enlightenment the same way everyone has the inborn ability for logical reasoning. It just needs to be cultivated.

An important thing to note is that practices, constructs, and concepts, exposed in this book, are reflecting experiences of a man. Since woman's brain, physiology, and body have a somewhat differ-

[7] *śrīpūrvaśāstre tatproktaṃ tarko yogāṅgamuttamam* TA.4.15.a

ent morphology and function, it is not clear that these techniques would work as well for women.

Attitudes

When I pushed forward,
I was whirled about.
When I stayed in place,
I sank.

Oghatarana Sutta

One does not pursue enlightenment out of fancy, for the path is torturous, the goal uncertain,[8] and the will to advance treacherous. *Sādhana* is at times brutal, even when its fruits are blissful. Therefore, the first requisite condition for any serious practice is a firm resolve.

Next, the real motive behind the initial pursuit of enlightenment, is rarely enlightenment itself. So, it is important to make one's *sādhana* attuned to that motive. Here is Buddha's advice:[9]

> One should not neglect one's own quest by adopting a quest of another, however great. Having come to full understanding of one's own quest, one has a chance to pursue the quest for what is real.

Attaining "what is real" is "the prime necessity of every human life" [Ram82].

Another major factor of progress is the will to contemplate. As said in *Śivasūtra*,

> Realization of the Truth comes from the will to contemplate.[10] He, who realized the Truth, lives in complete freedom.[11]

Sometimes, when one knows exactly what to contemplate and how to do it, this "will to contemplate" is absent. The source of the "will to contemplate" is knowledge, obtained from direct experience.[12]

[8]What is sought is unknown in details untill it is found.

[9]DhP.166

[10]*dhīvaśāt sattvasiddhiḥ* ShS.III.12

[11]*siddhaḥ svatantrabhāvaḥ* ShS.III.13

[12]This requires some explanation. There is a gap between watching live demonstrations of practices or being able to verbally describe them, and the actual performance of practices that brings results. In the course of practice,

Next, one should be following some reasonable criteria for correctness and relevancy of practices. These criteria are specific to the technique used and to one's disposition, and change with time. Overall, if practices are effective then many reactions, including some belonging to the autonomic nervous system, become less automatic. Successful practices should result in less reactivity in general and should lead to the Unknown, providing experiences of amazement and wonder; practice results should be robust and lasting, even after the practice ends. A good criteria is formed by recollecting a state of mind as close as possible to the goal of a particular practice, and using that recollected state as a mark, proximity to which is the criterion. If practice is relevant to one's current stage, then perceptible and intended changes should be apparent in three months at most.

Another important attitude is the personal preciousness of freedom. If absent, many practices will lack proper motivation. In the course of a *sādhana* this preciousness will only increase.

Do not expect *sādhana* to become a safe harbor or a refuge from the world. If one thinks of *sādhana* as an escape from the "slings and arrows of outrageous fortune," then the friuts will likely be very limited. The spiritual path helps one to cope with "outrageous fortune" without escaping it. One indicator of an effective practice is being on the edge of the Unknown and facing problems that one would prefer to avoid.

one constantly faces uncertainty and confusion, especially while engaged in analytical practices. When this happens, the philosophical system provides paradigms and principles that point out where and how further efforts should be applied, but it does not supply the will to actually do it. It is one's own experience that provides crucial particular details, instrumentation, and concentration of willpower, that bridge that gap. Maintaining a journal makes one's own experiences readily available.

What should be avoided:

> any activity or practice that makes one oblivious or less sensitive to cognitive and emotional dissonances, though it might lead to a blissful abiding;[13]
>
> joining any cult or being frequently exposed to a cult;[14]
>
> making *sādhana* a part of ego or a social role;
>
> taking any philosophical system as "the one and only true system of liberation";[15]
>
> secret doctrines or practices;[16]
>
> overreliance on empowerments, initiations and blessings, for these might convey, in addition to the benefits they confer, the message, "You are not self-sufficient. There is something that should be given to you." In the *Pratyabhijña* system this message is considered to be wrong.

---

[13]Exposure to dissonances without means to cope with them is not generally beneficial; rather, one should try to expand the spectrum of conflicts and dissonances that one is capable of coping with. There are many positive sides to being sensitive to dissonances. One of them is the ability to follow the Middle path. Another is an opportunity to eliminate *vikalpa*-s.

[14]Cults are not necessarily religious. Among their common characteristics are: exclusivity that leads to progressive social and/or intellectual isolation; supression of critical thinking, that is substituted by a group-think; sharp and rigid boundaries between members of the cult and outside society, that lead to "us" vs. "them" group dynamic; a set of "truths" that each member is obliged to believe are evident.

[15]Such belief causes resistance to using techniques and concepts from other systems that at times might be more relevant to one's needs.

[16]One sometimes reads in ancient scriptures that this or that practice is "secret." What is often meant by "secret" is that even if one reads a description of some practice or observes it, but does not possess the experiential layer of meaning required to understand and benefit from the practice, then the true meaning of what was read or observed remain hidden, or "secret." But it is not a "secret," that is maintained by a conspiracy of the initiated. As Swami Muktananda wrote, "Your path should be one that is open to everyone."

The other meaning of the term "secret" in scriptures is that a practice is "hidden" by layers of preliminary practices, without mastering of which the practice might be injurious.

चितिः स्वतन्त्रा विश्वसिद्धिहेतुः ॥ १॥

स्वेच्छया स्वभित्तौ विश्वमुन्मीलयति ॥ २॥

तन्नाना अनुरूपग्राह्यग्राहकभेदात् ॥ ३॥

चितिसंकोचात्मा चेतनोऽपि संकुचितविश्वमयः ॥ ४॥

चितिरेव चेतनपदादवरूढा चेत्यसंकोचिनी चित्तम् ॥ ५॥

तन्मयो मायाप्रमाता ॥ ६॥

स चैको द्विरूपस्त्रिमयश्चतुरात्मा सप्तपञ्चकस्वभावः ॥ ७॥

तद्भूमिकाः सर्वदर्शनस्थितयः ॥ ८॥

चिद्वत्तच्छक्तिसंकोचात् मलावृतः संसारी ॥ ९॥

तथापि तद्वत्पञ्चकृत्यानि करोति ॥ १०॥

आभासनरक्तिविमर्शनबीजावस्थापनविलापनतस्तानि ॥ ११॥

तदपरिज्ञाने स्वशक्तिभिर्व्यामोहितता संसारित्वम् ॥ १२॥

तत्परिज्ञाने चित्तमेव अन्तर्मुखीभावेन चेतनपदाध्यारोहात् चितिः ॥ १३॥

चितिवह्निरवरोहपदे छन्नोऽपि मात्रया मेयेन्धनं प्लुष्यति ॥ १४॥

बललाभे विश्वमात्मसात्करोति ॥ १५॥

चिदानन्दलाभे देहादिषु चेत्यमानेष्वपि चिदैकात्म्यप्रतिपत्तिदार्ढ्यं
जीवन्मुक्तिः ॥ १६॥

मध्यविकासाच्चिदानन्दलाभः ॥ १७॥

विकल्पक्षयशक्तिसंकोचविकासवाहच्छेदाद्यन्तकोटिनिभालनादय
इहोपायाः ॥ १८॥

समाधिसंस्कारवति व्युत्थाने भूयोभूयश्चिदैक्यामर्शान्नित्योदित
समाधिलाभः ॥ १९॥

तदा प्रकाशानन्दसारमहामन्त्रवीर्यात्मकपूर्णाहन्तावेशात्
सदा सर्वसर्गसंहारकारिनिजसंविद्देवताचक्रेश्वरताप्राप्तिर्
भवतीति शिवम् ॥ २०॥

Sanskrit text of the *Pratyabhijñāhṛdayam*.

Concepts

> ...those who do not observe
> the movements of their own
> minds must of necessity
> be unhappy.
>
> *Marcus Aurelius*

The formulation of the *Pratyabhijñā* system presented here is attributed to Kshemaraja. It is very short — 20 sentences — and fits onto one page (see the opposite page).

Many concepts of the system, describing mind/cognition are of a dynamic, of a movement. Herein is a difficulty of both describing and understanding these concepts. In order to become perceptible, that dynamic has to be projected onto some material substratum. For example, to explain the concept of "falling" one shows falling objects — an apple, a stone, a feather, etc. Understanding this explanation requires one to abstract the observed falling of an apple, a stone, a feather, etc., from a particlar object falling, from the time it takes for it to fall, from the place it is falling into, from the cause of the fall, and so on. Only then might the abstract concept of falling be understood. The same way, understanding of the highly abstract concepts of Kashmir Shaivism philosophical systems requires abstraction of the observable dynamics of mental phenomena from the content or the substratum of that dynamic. In each case, such a process of systematic abstraction is left to the practitioner.

Below is a vocabulary of concepts required for understanding everything that follows. It should be noted that the basic concepts of this philosophical system are undefined, for they are not reducible to other concepts (the same way the concepts of a point, a line and a plane are undefined in the Euclidean geometry). However, since it might be easier to form in one's mind the correct ideas behind words with the help of approximations, I've attempted to formulate such approximations based on my own experiences.

All such approximations are made on the experiential plane of meaning, since all concepts and propositions of this system have but one goal — to aid in the process of self transformation with the ultimate goal of liberation.

Many terms in this vocabulary occur in other philosophical systems. At times, their meaning is quite different from system to system, which might contribute to confusion. Only meanings used in the *Pratyabhijñā* system are pointed at in here.

In Trika, many concepts are presented as a projection of the triad *jñāna, kriyā, icchā* (approximately translated as "perception, activity, desire"). Therefore, some of the concepts have a triple definition, one for each member of the triad.

In some cases, a definition is given by means of several expressions, separated with semicolon. The reader should try to form a concept that is "in the middle" of all those expressions, with the expectation that the resulting concept will be non-verbal.

The order of terms is non-alphabetical, but such that any definition refers, as a rule, only to definitions prior to it.

prakāśa is that which manifests itself in every mental phenomenon;
energy that is the carrier of all stimulation,[17] whether because of sensory input, memory or imagination;
substratum of all sense-datum;
that which always (at all times and in all cases) illuminates[18] (as opposed to having other substance to illuminate).

The concept of *prakāśa* is central to formulation of many concepts of Trika: Tantraloka even gives condition for liberation, quoting Yogacara, as "liberation comes from illumination of everything."[19]

This illumination is inherent in one's being. As Buddha

[17]The term "stimulation," as used here, is understood to mean immediate causes of activation of mental things; light falling onto light receptors in the eye, the energy of concentration that allows one to imagine non-existing things, the power of association that brings memories to mind — all these are examples of stimulation. It should be noted that stimulation might be below the threshold of perception.

[18]*prakāśonāma yaścāyaṃsarvatraiva prakāśate* TA.1.54.a

[19]*uktaṃ ca śrīyogācāre mokṣaḥ sarvaprakāśanāt* TA.6.58.b

said,[20] "Luminous is the mind."

jñeya what is to be experienced;
potential or actual object of experience;
localized expression of *prakāśa*.

jñāna perception, experience (in the broadest sense);
the process of establishing relation between the subject and objects of perception.

grāhya sense-datum as the transition between manifested/non-manifested state of stimuli, of the energy of mental actions or of emotions, desires, urges, etc.;
above-threshold change in the intensity of *prakāśa*.

Though *jñeya* might be stable, corresponding to it *grāhya* might be variable. The reason for this is that only the changes in stimulation are perceived. Therefore, in order to perceive static stimuli, there should be co-occuring instability.[21]

grāhaka a process of establishing relation between *grāhya* and a perceiver (see *pramātṛ* below).

prameya a stream of sense-datum in general (as opposed to mere manifestation, as in *grāhya*). The major difference between *prameya* and *grāhya* is that temporal extension of *prameya* greatly exceeds the interval of perceptual integration.

mātṛ a specific mental process that measures, apportions or evaluates.

Notice that *mātṛ* is *the arising* of an opinion, judgement, adjustment, etc., not the opinion, judgment, etc., itself.

It is important to understand that there is no entity that measures, apportions or evaluates;[22] there is only a process, which is nothing but a specific dynamic in the *prakāśa*.

[20] Pabhassara Sutta, AN 1.49

[21] To provide this instability is a basic function of the organs of perception (for example, saccadic movements of the eyes).

[22] like a Homunculus

For example, in the domain of perception, an arising of any opinion that might be expressed with words like "this color looks more blue than green," "this is not the same smell as usual," "this tea is hot," is an example of a *mātṛ*.

In the domain of actions, selection of force of a throw so that this very pebble hits that very rock, or modulation of voice so that it becomes a whisper, or tapping a finger in synch with music — are all examples of a *mātṛ*.

In the domain of desires, an arising of judgements like "a bit of salt — is exactly what I wanted," "this tea is too hot," "this girl is lovely," "this is to be avoided" is an example of a *mātṛ*.

māna an opinion, an evaluation, an adjustment that is a result of a *mātṛ*.

It is strongly influenced by *pramātṛ*-s: "An opinion, an evaluation is contrived, fixed by preexisting *pramātṛ*-s".[23] As a consequence of this influence, there is no "pure" perception, or seeing of only what is there to be seen, and, therefore, opinions based on perceptions are always distorted.

pramātṛ is a mental construct, appearing as an independent source of *prakāśa*.[24]

It is an active filter of *prameya* that:

1. accentuates/attenuates reflected *prakāśa*;

2. organizes *prameya*-s into sequences, arrays, and gradations;

3. provides context for *prameya*-s by means of augmentation.

At any given moment there might be more than one *pramātṛ* active. They accomplish distortion of *prameya*-s by the means of 1–3 listed above on a subconscious level, primarily because of the high speed of those processes.

[23] *mānataiva tu sā prācyapramātṛparikalpitā* TA.3.128.a
[24] *pramātṛtā svatantratvarūpā seyaṃ prakāśate* TA.10.269.a

One of the effects of a *pramātṛ* is *saṃjñā* — augmentation and discarding of features of impressions in order to make them agree with expectations or prior impressions.[25]

meya — aspects of *prameya* that are to be evaluated by a *mātṛ*; *prameya*, put in a context by a *pramātṛ* for a *mātṛ*.

pramāna — sense-datum (from *prameya*), filtered, augmented, and put into a context by *pramātṛ*-s in a way that makes possible an evaluation of the *prameya* by a *mātṛ* (that is, it makes possible the production of *māna*);
sense-datum when used as a source of knowledge.

mati — procedural knowledge;
mental gesture;
functional attitude;
resolve.

mati is a knowledge that is, at the same time, a continuous action. Thus, it is not verbal, since it ought to be on the *paśyanti* level of speech.

viśva — the whole of the "mental" things;
the Universe as reflected in one's being;
the intellectual faculty to make everything subject to cognition.

ātman — an autonomous instance that is possessing of cyclic transformations (for example, a being that is breathing);
that which gives unity to a composite.

When used in non-technical sense, *ātman* here means "self."

vāyu — a subtle energy;
a dynamic of activation of specific neurotransmitters in various parts of the nervous system;
a wave of expression of specific neurotransmitters.

According to *Śivasvarodaya*,[26] there are 10 types of subtle energies: *prāṇa, apāna, samāna, udāna, vyāna, nāga, kūrma, kṛkala, devadatta, dhanañjaya*.

[25] See commentary to *sūtra* 8.
[26] ShSv.42-47

prāṇa is predominant at the moment the breathing in starts;
apāna is predominant at the moment the breathing out starts;
samāna is predominant in the process of digestion;
udāna — in energy surge through *suṣumnā* when *prāṇa* and *apāna* are in equilibrium;
vyāna — in the state of *samādhi*. It is felt as pervading everything. It makes maintaining *āsana* and other functions of the body effortless during hours of remaining in *samādhi*.

nāga manifests itself during vomiting;
kūrma is predominant in blinking of eyes;
kṛkala — in sneezing;
devadatta — in yawning;
dhanañjaya keeps integrity of the physical body after death (and is probably a source of the notion "zombie").

A *vāyu* might be perceived as "inner flow" or "touch" or "cloud of sensation" in some parts of the body, especially when the flow is interrupted or obstructed. Sensations might differ from person to person, but what is important is that flows of the vital energies might be perceived and even controlled. *Prāṇāyāma* is a set of practices that accomplishes just such control. For a practical guidance on *prāṇāyāma*, see [SR98] and [Iye99].

prāṇa the *vāyu*, or subtle energy, that is predominant at the moment the breathing in starts.

It facilitates mental agitation and serves as "energetic background" for many processes. *Prāṇa* originates in *kanda* (a spot inside the body about five thumb widths below the navel)[27] and is transmutated into other *vāyu*-s. The importance of the control of *prāṇa* for a philosophical inquiry and for any yogic practice comes from the close connection between psychological processes and flows of *prāṇa*, and between *prāṇa* and physiological processes. Control over *prāṇa* is a prerequisite for control over the mind. Strong disequilibrium

[27] *prāṇaḥ kandāt prabhṛtyeva tathāpyatra na susphuṭaḥ* TA.6.49

in *prāṇa* distribution is a source of errors in reasoning, especially in operations on ill-defined concepts.

nāḍī channel, along which *vāyu*-s flow. It is not necessarily a physical channel like a nerve or a vein, but a persistent pattern of neurotransmitter expression. These patterns are called "channels" because they are felt that way. There are many thousands of *nāḍī* throughout the body. Of them three are the most important for any yogic practice: *iḍā*, *piṅgalā*, and *suṣumnā*.

cakra an intersection of three or more *nāḍī*-s. When flows of subtle energies are obstructed, *cakra* might be felt as a spot about thumb-width in size. The "petals" of a *cakra* are experienced as sensations of directional flows to/from the central spot of the *cakra*. Different numbers of *cakra*-s are recognized by different traditions, but six *cakra*-s are recognized universally. For details on *nāḍī*-s, *cakra*-s, "petals", etc., see [SR98].

devatā spontaneous unpredictability that has a potential to overwhelm.

It is usually translated as "a divinity," which is also correct, albeit vague.

karma lasting aftereffects of an action, physical or mental (especially of an intent), that disturbs equilibrium of some configuration either in the cognitive or in the emotional spheres, or in the sphere of activity.

For example, "ills" that one mentally does or intends to do to others continue to live inside as tormenting phantoms. These intentions are reflected back as apparitions in auditory, tactile, proprioceptive, and gustatory modalities. Such reflections are primarily perceptible during wakeful dreaming (the state of transition between dreaming and wakefulness).

An example of *karma* in the cognitive sphere: a definite verbal answer to the question, which of these two colors is closer to that one when both of the colors are equally (in individual color space) similar to the third color, will result in the inclination to perceive in the future those colors as unequally similar to the third. It is the intention to see the difference that expressed itself in an answer that will have lasting effects.

Here are examples of *karma* in the emotional sphere.

Suppose that a person steals your pocket money. If you become intent on inflicting some pain on that person then the personal significance of money would become much greater than before, thus promoting greed and selfishness in the long run. If your were to harm that person in reality, those effects would be even stronger.

Suppose you experience jealousy because some hunk is dancing with your girl. Intention to compete with your rival nurtures aspirations to be like him, thus creating a conflict within — for you still intend to compete. If you act according to this intention, the ensuing internal conflict will be all the more intense.

Suppose that you undertake to solve a difficult problem in some area with the intention to become the very best in that area. This intention to be the best will cause resistance to becoming aware of others' significant contributions to the solution of the same problem.

Suppose that whenever you are having a difficult question, you go to your teacher for an answer. The lasting effect of going to your teacher for answers is to diminish self-reliance and to lessen the ability to investigate and to research on your own.

Here is an example of *karma* in the sphere of action.

An attempt to imitate a new sound with phonemes of your mother tounge causes you to perceive that sound to be much closer to those phonemes than it actually is.

Another example: If the only kind of *yoga* you were to practice for extended periods of time were *hatha*, then it would make you too obsessed about your own body and put in place ideas of purity–impurity that are too restrictive for effective practice.[28]

[28]Compare with
kiṃcijjñair yā smṛtā śuddhiḥ sā aśuddhiḥ śambhudarśane
na śucir hyaśucistasmānnirvikalpaḥ sukhī bhavet VBh.123
"What is taught by those whose knowledge is sporadic as being purified, is not purified at all, from the point of view of this system. This is so,

The best action is that which leaves no traces, that is, it is *karma*-free, for *karma* is created by acting or intending to act beyond what is required by the situation.

Karma is neither absolute determinism, nor the will of God, nor a random conglomeration of circumstances.[29] If you throw a pebble above your head and it falls down and hits you, this is not the law of karma at work, but laws of physics.

How strong the aftereffects are, and what the practical consequences of their existence will be, is not deterministic. Rather, it depends on many other things, particularly, on how spiritually advanced one is.[30] Whether *karma* is deemed positive or negative depends on whether it reduces or strengthens *vikalpa*-s.

Karma has the potential to cause physical illness: an intention, even if not yet expressed, might cause lasting changes in flows of *prāṇa*, *apāna*, etc.; lasting changes in such flows cause, with time, physiological disfunctions, and those might lead to an illness.

saṃvid — the cognitive faculty to establish correspondence, coherence, or continuity between what appear to be separate entities;
prakāśa of meaning, of intent or of content.

For example, recognizing an object as perceived before involves establishing correspondence between memory of the object and the current percept of it. This correspondence is established by *saṃvid* (since any two perceptual streams from the same object are always somewhat different). When finding a difference between a pair of images, the basis of the comparison is established by *saṃvid*. When interpreting an unclear image as some definite thing, *saṃvid* establishes identity between the thing and the image. When drawing an unfamiliar symbol, the coherence of muscular activity to the perceptual image being drawn is sustained by *saṃvid*.

because in comparison with the state of *bhairava*, nothing is more pure than it is impure, and nothing is more impure than it is pure.
Only when one is devoid of *vikalpa*-s, one might become happy."

[29] Tittha Sutta AN.III.61

[30] Lonaphala Sutta AN.III.99, Sivaka Sutta SN.XXXVI.21

The source of this ability to unify disparate entities is *parāsaṃvid*, or the ultimate *saṃvid*, which is *cit*.

sattva — luminosity, differentiating real from unreal;
source of attachment to happiness and knowledge.[31]

rajas — transience;[32]
source of passion and attachment to action.[33]

tamas — inertia, resistance to change;
source of attachment to delusions.[34]

guṇa — a pervasive attribute, one of the three: *sattva*, *rajas*, or *tamas*.[35]

aṇu — a form of *śiva* that is a non-particularised *prakāśa*, augmented with *icchāśakti*, *jñānaśakti*, and *kriyāśakti*, and in which the inherent bliss has dwindled,
and in which *śiva*, out of his own free will, is causing the individual "self" to appear limited.[36]

To possess the form of *aṇu* is to be rigidly defined by what is desirable and what is undesirable, by what is known/experienced and what is unknown/unexperienced, by what is doable and what is not doable. Genuine creativity and existential being are a step beyond the limits of *aṇu*.

An important practice is to recognize an everyday idea of "self" as having the form of *aṇu*. Just observe and make notice of limitations and boundaries you set when functionally defining "self." Notice ideas you do not dare to think or to speak of, but that have a chance of being true; notice endeavors you do not dare to pursue, but deep in your heart would like to, and notice what you prefer not to see, hear, smell, taste, or touch for no apparent and strong *reason*.

---

[31] *sattvaṃ sukhe sañjayati...* BhG XIV.9.a
[32] *... rajaḥ karmaṇi bhārata* BhG XIV.9.a
[33] *rajo rāgātmakaṃ viddhi tṛṣṇāsāṅgasamudbhavam* BhG XIV.7.a
[34] *jñānamāvṛtya tu tamaḥ pramāde sañjayatyuta* BhG XIV.9.b
[35] *sattvaṃ rajastama iti guṇāḥ prakṛtisambhavāḥ* BhG XIV.5.a
[36] *... icchājñānakriyāśaktiyuktaḥanavacchinnaḥprakāśonijānandaviśrāntaḥ śivarūpaḥsa evasvātantryādātmānaṃsaṃkucitamavabhāsayannaṇuriti...* AbhTs.1.5

In the emotional sphere the state of *aṇu* is characterized as "being driven by the waves of emotions, conditioned by memories."

When one is able to transcend the state of *aṇu* then

> Desirable things[37] don't charm the mind,
> undesirable ones[38] bring no resistance.[39]

This maxim not only describes the result, but points to a means to go beyond *aṇu* in the emotional sphere. These four dimensions — material gain/loss, honor/disgrace, praise/censure, and phisiological pleasure/pain — encompass many factors that, by acquiring the status of an imperative (like "strive for praise", "evade censure"), make "self" into a puppet manipulated by strings, thus diminishing the bliss of self-will. Though by following such an imperative automatically, pleasure might be gained and pain avoided, there is no bliss in the pleasure and no peace in the absence of pain. One of the important points of the *Pratyabhijñā* system is that these "strings" are just expressions of one's own will that are devoid of awareness and self-reflection. Accurate recollection of those expressions of one's own will, that became such strings or chains, is the first step to reconfiguring them.

Here is an effective practice, based on this maxim. It lessens the "being driven by the waves of emotions, conditioned by memories." The practice has five steps:

1. Recollect and write down extreme cases of each of the four dimensions in as many personal details as possible.
2. Recognize in everyday activities transitions (decisions, associations, arising of activity, cessation of activity) that are automatic (or almost automatic) and are motivated/energized by an affinity with items from step 1.[40]

[37] gain, status, praise, pleasure
[38] loss, disgrace, censure, pain
[39] AN 8.6 Lokavipatti Sutta, translated by Thanissaro Bhikkhu
[40] The interruption of transition by means of meditative relaxation of effort is likely to bring the relevant item to the fore of attention.

3. Once a transition and the items it has affinity with are recognized, make the affinities as neutral as possible by two actions: by retracting the resolve to strive for or to evade situations associated with each of the items that the transition is motivated by; and then by challenging the strength of the affinity. The challenge is accomplished by finding reasons why the strong affinity is not actually as good as was believed, or assumed, at the time of its formation,[41] and with finding how more neutral affinity with the item is beneficial with respect to other personal values.
4. Having accomplished step 3 for the most pervasive transitions, return to the item on the list from step 1, retract the resolve to strive (beyond what is required by reason) for the attainment if it is a positive item, or do resolve not to run from or resist it (beyond what is required by reason) if it is a negative one.
5. Form pairs of opposite items from step 1. Then, for each pair, perform special *pūjā*, described below.

The *pūjā* is done in this case in the following manner.[42] Bring both situations, making a pair of opposites, into attention focus, and try to become absorbed into both of them simultanuously. Successful absorption is marked by a sense of being in a great void space. Then, find *mati* that is relatively stable in the neutral spot between both opposites, stable despite shifting emphasis of moderate strength on one opposite case vs. another (the emphasis is created by varying concentration on one item, while still being absorbed into both). Maintain the *mati* active, while being absorbed into both opposites and while emphasis is shifting between them, for at least 10 mininutes — to make the *mati* stable. In order to have a lasting effect, the *mati* should be guiding one's behaviour outside this practice.

[41] A significant reduction in the level of awareness is almost always a strong reason, when awareness is high on the scale of personal values.

[42] *pūjā nāma na puṣpādyairyā matiḥ kriyate dṛḍhā |*
nirvikalpe mahāvyomni sā pūjā hyādarāllayaḥ || VBh.147

There is no need to make a single exhaustive list during step 1. Just a few items that seem related will suffice. As soon as one's awareness is expanded enough to allow the same treatment of new items, the practice might be repeated with a new list.

The are five major problems to overcome for making this practice useful:

a. difficulty with becoming aware of the extreme cases and of the transitions which, by being almost automatic, are hard to detect;

b. difficulty with attending to the cases and to the transitions long enough to perform analysis;

c. difficulty with not being carried away by the emotional influence of the recollected situations;

d. difficulty with becoming absorbed into both opposite cases simultaneously;

e. difficulty with finding an adequate *mati* that is ethical and does not contradict major postulates and rules of the adopted philosophical system.

To deal with problem a., a systematic interruption and analysis of habitual actions and meditation are helpful. To deal with problem b., concentration practices (*dhāraṇa* and *dhyāna*) or any activity requiring long chains of non-automatic mental operations are recommended. To deal with problem c., one could cultivate the attitude of being just an observer. For problem d., start by calm breathing in and out with alternate concentration on corresponding "positive" and "negative" cases. At the same time, raise the level of attention on other than current case untill both levels of attention are about the same. To deal with problem e., a thorough knowledge of this philosophical system and philosophy in general are of great help.

vikalpa a state of polarization that makes anything manifested to be defined on a X–not-X scale.

In the emotional sphere, *vikalpa* of X is born of deprivation, resulting from the lack of expedients to satisfy a particular desire X. Such *vikalpa* is made very stable by the resolve of the inherent in one's self free will to satisfy X.[43]

Vikalpa is in opposition to recognizing primordial unity of own self. It is an obstacle to *yoga*.[44]

In the sphere of perception/cognition: *vikalpa* is an ascertainment, casting duality.[45] *Vikalpa* is that which, having inhibited the fact of the selectivity of attention by means of *māyā*, projects itself as the disjunction between what is manifested and the unmanifested counterpart of the manifested.[46]

It projects the duality onto the body, onto vital energies (*vāyu*-s), onto perception and imagination, making everything appear as if in a cloud — the perspective is very limited but what restricts it can not be seen — expressing *vimarśa* through a contrast between what it makes into opposites by manifesting one and rejecting the other. *Vikalpa* is an expression of "I am" through contrasts.

In the sphere of activity: *vikalpa*-s manifest themselves as synchronous contraction/relaxation of complimentary muscle groups,[47] as tides of breathing in and out, when waning of *prāṇa* is synchronized with waxing of *apāna*.

It is through using *vikalpa*-s that personal likes–dislikes, emotions, and affective states of mind pervade all of the Universe, as reflected in one's being. As soon as there is indefiniteness, it becomes amalgamated with various likes–dislikes. In the course of practicing detachment and dispassion (*vairagya*, as understood in Yoga Sutra — complete understanding of how the world, observed directly or known through literary tradition, subjugates one's will — when such understanding is born of a re-

[43] *vikalpaḥ kasyacit svātmasvātantryād eva susthiraḥ |*
upāyāntarasāpekṣyaviyogenaiva jāyate || TA.5.3

[44] *kasyacittu vikalpo'sau svātmasaṃskaraṇaṃ prati* TA.5.4.a

[45] *nāsau vikalpaḥ sa hyukto dvayākṣepī viniścayaḥ* IPK.1.6.1.cd

[46] *cittattvaṃ māyayā hitvā bhinna evāvabhāti yaḥ*
dehe buddhāvatha prāṇe kalpite nabhasīva vā
pramātṛtvenāhamiti vimarśo'nyavyapohanāt
vikalpa eva sa parapratiyogyavabhāsajaḥ IPK.1.6.4-5

[47] If the bicep is contracted, the tricep is automatically relaxed.

duction in the thirst for desirable things[48]), which is an essential component of any *sādhana*, this amalgamation disappears, uncovering the indefiniteness of experience and of being as such. That is why it was said that the progress in *yoga* is marked by amazement.[49]

Diminution of *vikalpa*-s is an important set of practices of this system (see *sūtra* 18).

Diminution of *vikalpa*-s in the sphere of actions would be manifested as a natural gap between waning of *apāna* and the surge of *prāṇa*, and as between waning of *prāṇa* and the surge of *apāna*. These gaps are known as "space between breaths."

To make this gap long enough, practise *prāṇāyāma*-s.

Another manifestation of the diminution of *vikalpa*-s in the sphere of actions is that *āsana*-s become effortless and comfortable.[50] Thus, practice *āsana*-s, especially those that are symmetrical.

In the sphere of perception/cognition, the diminution is done by a variety of techniques, for example: "If one were to form in mind an image of all space directions, as they are given in the sensations of the body, [and spread the attention evenly to all six of them — up, down, right, left, front and back], then, when his mind becomes devoid of polarizations, everything "his" would be vanishing."[51]

Here are other examples from the *Vijñānabhairava* tantra: "If one were to cause the void in the very top of the head, the void in the *mūladhāra* and the void in the *anāhata* appear with stability; then, at that moment, from absense of polarization in subtle body, arises the absense of *vikalpa*-s in the mind."[52]

An important technique for reducing *vikalpa*-s in the sphere of perceptions is the analysis of experiences in terms of *tattva*-s, followed by conscious withdrawal of

---

[48] *dṛṣṭānuśravikaviṣayavitṛṣṇasyavaśīkārasaṃjñāvairāgyam* YS.I.15

[49] *vismayoyogabhūmikāḥ* ShS.I.12

[50] *sthirasukham āsanam* YS.II.46

[51] *nijadehe sarvadikkaṃ yugapad bhāvayed viyat* |
nirvikalpamanās tasya viyat sarvam pravartate || VBh.43

[52] *pṛṣṭhaśūnyaṃ mūlaśūnyaṃ hṛcchūnyam bhāvayet sthiram* |
yugapan nirvikalpatvān nirvikalpodayas tataḥ || VBh.45

attentional and intentional support to various *tattva*-s and imagining the same experiences without them. A good example of such imagining is given by the painting by Salvador Dali "Infinite Enigma." Chanting *Om̃*, while paying attention to smooth, barely noticable transitions between *a*, *u*, *ṃ* and all gradations of the *anusvara* (*ṃ*) to the final silence, is a practice for reducing *vikalpa*-s in the auditory modality.

In the emotional sphere the diminution is done by practicing *vairagya*, by resolving to search alternative ways to satisfy a strong desire X, by mentally delaying the moment when the desire "just ought to be satisfied," imagining how to live without this desire being satisfied and still being content (if possible).

The most important techinique for reduction of *vikalpa*-s in the emotional sphere is the analysis using the paradigms of the five acts and of the three *mala*-s (see *sūtra* 10 and entry for *mala*).

puruṣa pure self-awareness, having no agency, devoid of *guṇa*-s, without any ideo-motoric dynamic, exempt from all modalities of perception and of all types of ideas (see the entry for *mahābhūta*-s);[53]
consciousness as observer of self-reflection in the void.

prakṛti biological infrastructure of a being;
the totality of biological programs that prime, drive, or modulate psychological processes.

prakṛti has three *guṇa*-s: *sattva*, *rajas* and *tamas*.

Examples of biological programs are:
- flight-or-fight reaction;
- long-term potentiation;
- the cycle of wakefulness, dreaming, and deep sleep;
- development of abstract thinking;
- establishing of and participation in social hierarchies and networks;
- desire for power over other humans;
- gender roles;
- kin selection.

[53] *karaṇendriyahīnaśca bhūtatanmātravarjitaḥ* |
akartā nirguṇaścāhaṃ cinmātraḥ puruṣaḥ smṛtaḥ || SvaT.12.75

There are many other programs.

An important assumption of the *Pratyabhijñā* system (and of many other philosophical systems of ancient India) is that this biological infrastructure is not determinative of psychological processes, but is merely slanting them by providing the path of least resistance.

Very important for many practices in here is a set of biological programs related to social hierarchies and networks. For details, see Appendix A.

buddhi the cognitive faculty of forming, applying, and manipulating knowledge;
the faculty of reasoning and establishing certainty.

The Bhagavad Gita states the importance of *buddhi* in this way: "what is defined as happiness beyond any limit is beyond perception, and is to be grasped by *buddhi*."[54]

Buddhi deals with concepts that are knowledge, not notions. Notions are constructs of *manas* and are merely loose associations of several mental constructs.

There is a very important difference between concepts that are knowledge and those that are notions. Definitness of notions is derived from perceptual similarity (expressed by "It seems that way"), while that of knowledge is from procedural measurement, based on the most sharp of perceptual distinctions, (expressed by "The measure is such").

Knowledge might exist without having any counterpart in perceptual experiences, like in case of mathematical constructs, or even in contradiction to perceptions, like in cases of visual illusions.

An example demonstrating the difference between notions and knowledge is a well known experiment by J. Piage. Take two jars of transparent glass, one short but with a large square foundation, another very tall but with a small square foundation, both having the same volume. Take two identical glasses, each having the same volume as the jars, and fill them with water. Since the glasses are the same, the question, "which one

[54] *sukhamātyantikaṃ yattadbuddhigrāhyamatīndriyam* BhG 6.21.a

has more water?" is easily decided on the basis of perceptual similarity. Next, pour water from the glasses into the jars. Now, the same question, if answered on the basis of a notion, will likely yield the response "The tall one." If the knowledge of preservation of the volume of liquids were the basis of the response, the answer would be "Both have the same amount of water." Though the employment of a notion instead of knowledge in this case is exhibited mostly by children, in more complex situations arising during introspection, it is a common occurence.

A notion is quite easily morphed by strong emotions, because judgments of perceptual similarity are. On the other hand, knowledge is only slightly affected by even strong emotions, because procedural measurements are such. The purest form of knowledge is mathematics. Even if one is tempted to find that the sum of the interior angles of a triangle is less than 180 degree, (such temptation might arise, for example, in case of social coersion — if everyone around gets this result), the procedure of obtaining a mathematical proof would yield the correct result.

The difference between notions and knowledge also manifests itself in dealing with contradictions. When contradiction arises, if notions are employed, then the contradiction is resolved by either omission of a premise or by stretching boundaries of some notions. On the other hand, if knowledge is employed, it forces one to search for false premises.

Whenever a judgment is generated by a vague sense of "it seems OK," or "it feels OK," or by a sense of emotional or cognitive dissonance, it is likely to be the result of a notion. In this case an appearance of certainty is derived from the strength of like/dislike attitudes.

Whenever a judgment is generated by a procedure, it is likely to be the result of a knowledge, and its certainty is derived from the degree of universality of that procedure.

Thinking with notions is guided by avoidance of cognitive and emotional dissonance. Thinking with knowledge is directed by logic and procedures.

Generalizations, induction, verbal formulations, and extrapolations usually lead to notions. In order to elevate a notion to the level of knowledge, it must be augmented with a procedure having definite conditions of applicability. This means that all definitions given here will, under the best circumstances, give rise to notions; these notions might be transformed into knowledge by practical application aimed at making them procedural. Such transformation of notions into knowledge should be a part of any *sādhana*.

Unfortunately, the field of introspection does not afford measurement procedures or a factual knowledge base of any substantial size, since memories are subject to filtration, re-casting, and a variety of interpretations. Here are some operations that approach the status of a measurement procedure:

noticing that something was/is present in the perceptual field;

noticing states of agitation, calm, desire, impulsiveness, etc.;

noticing a contradiction;

noticing that a particular idea/thing is in the field of attention;

directing attention towards something in particular;

concentrating the attention on something in particular;

inhibiting or suppressing of activation of some image/idea;

following an instruction;

applying a rule of logic.

The closest to procedural knowledge in this field are principles, paradigms, and scripts. A principle is not a mathematical law. It is an expression built with concepts as close to knowledge as possible, and it states a truth not easily derivable from observations, for observations are always incomplete and subject to diverging interpretations.

An example of a principle is the maxim from TA.15.236.b *ahantāyāṃ hi dehatvaṃ*, which states that "corporeality comes from consciousness *I am such* or *I intend to be such,*" and reflects, among other things, deep connection between volitional concept of self and physiological processes.[55]

A paradigm is a schema which defines a set of patterns to which phenomena would conform if properly analyzed. An example of a paradigm is The Four Noble Truths of Buddha. Another example of a paradigm is provided by the schema of the dependent co-arising (see *paṭiccasamuppādasutta* SN XII.1). Among paradigms of the *Pratyabhijñā* system are: 36 *tattva*-s (see below), the three *mala*-s (see below), *pañcakṛtyāni*, or the five acts (see sutra 10).

A script is a well defined sequence of actions. A simple but important example of a script is a formula for practicing a *dhāraṇa*, or concentration (directing mind to one place. YS.3.1 *deśabandhaścittasyadhāraṇā*) Here is the formula:

1. Choose a spot in a perceptual field (e.g., a symbol on a uniform background);
2. Direct all of the attention to that spot;
3. When distraction occurs, simply return the focus of attention to that spot;
4. Keep doing 2 and 3 for at least 20 minutes.

Buddhi is "colored" by the three *guṇa*-s. *Rajas* guides the manipulation of knowledge; it is manifest in the process of deduction. *Tamas* provides for recognition of fragments of the perceptual stream as compatible with certain knowledge. *Sattva* facilitates forming new knowledge.

ahaṃkāra the faculty of relating everything to "self"; the faculty of maintaining persistence of "I."

Ahaṃkāra is "colored" by the three *guṇa*-s. *Rajas* enables changes to personal boundaries; *tamas* is instrumental in maintaining "the unchangeable core of self"; *sattva* enables self-investigation and self-knowledge.

[55] A similar principle is part of the schema of dependent co-arising (see *paṭiccasamuppādasutta* SN XII.1), and states that becoming is a requisite condition of birth.

Ordinarily, *ahaṃkāra* is present in the waking state of mind the same way the nose is present in the field of visual perception. The nose provides a reference that defines some of the interpretation of visual stimuli. The same way, *ahaṃkāra* is present in the back of the mind and makes perception, thoughts and actions referenced to personal constructs (it makes them into *vikalpa*-s).

manas the "inner eye" that coordinates sensory inputs from different modalities and from the memory to ensure coherent experience;
the faculty of introspection that enables one to see arising and fading of ideas or images in one's mind;
the organ of perception that allows one to become aware of inner states, like sadness, joy, desire, aversion, etc.;
a stable area that is the hub of the mind's activity, and that provides a general framework for resolving indeterminancies and defines the general direction of activity.

antaḥkaraṇa (lit. "the inner instrument,") is the triad of *buddhi*, *ahaṃkāra* and *manas*. All components of the triad are structured and limited by *prakṛti* and, thus, are "colored" by the three *guṇa*-s: *sattva*, *rajas* or *tamas*.

The following concepts *cit*, *citi*, *vimarśa*, *svātantrya*, *śiva* and *śakti* are even less subject to definiton than others. Therefore, all "definitions" of them should be regarded only as pointers in certain contexts.

vimarśa shifting, non-uniform self-reflection, that is alternating between various degrees of affection and detachment.

svātantrya the freedom of will;
self-will.

svātantrya is a quality of *vimarśa*. From the perspective of action, it is defined as "the principal authorship and the supremacy to be such."[56]

The question of the existence of free will is central to many philosophical debates. There is no definite answer to this question that is convincingly established.

[56]comment to sutra 20 *svātantryamatha kartṛtvaṃ mukhyamīśvaratāpi ca*

The assumption of the existence of free will is expedient for the *Pratyabhijñā* system of liberation and, being conducive to efficient *sādhana*, is assumed here to be true. It seems that the contrary assumption of non-existence is, on the practical level, merely a declaration of the intent not to exercise this ability, despite it being manifest at least in some circumstances, be it through maintaining the comfort of drifting with the stream of *saṃsāra* or through the pain of venturing out of it.

camatkāra the aesthetic experience of the bliss of *svātantrya*.

citi long term facilitation of the ability to concentrate and to direct attention;
amplification/attetuation of attention;
fluid-like energy that, when self-contrasted, polarizes perception/cognition into duality "I"–"It".

This is the key concept of the *Pratyabhijñāhṛdayam* exposition of the *Pratyabhijñā* system.

What is meant here by "attention" is the general process of amplification/attetuation/selection of active, or to-become-active mental entities.

cit the Absolute, which is the substratum of all manifestation;
a pure perceptive attention that has two aspects — *prakāśa* and *vimarśa*.

It is also called *parāsaṃvid*, or the ultimate *saṃvid*.

Through *vimarśa*, *cit* possesses absolute free will (that is, *svātantrya*) and, therefore, *camatkāra*. *citi* is but a power of *cit*.

śiva *cit*, when the *vimarśa* aspect is emphasized;
the Absolute that spontanuously, like an infinitesimal pulsation, by the power of free will emanates the Universe as a self-reflection.

On a personal level, "being like *śiva*" means to be in the state of benevolent, happy tranquility, possessing unlimited creativity as a potentiality.

śakti unmodified by context, pure form of potentiality;
unmodified by context, pure form of transition;
infinitely elastic wave of energy.

> Various forms of *śakti* are projections of the basic form — that of "the spontaneous aspiration" of *śiva* to manifest the entire Universe.
>
> There are many forms, or projections, of *śakti*. All of them are qualities of *śiva*. The most fundamental for the *Pratyabhijñā* system are *icchāśakti*, *jñānaśakti*, *kriyāśakti* and *māyāśakti*.
>
> *śakti* is shaped or structured by a *mātṛ*.[57]

The two basic, and the most abstract, concepts of the *Pratyabhijñā* system are the concepts of *śiva* and *śakti*. *Śakti* is just a dynamic aspect of *śiva*. *Śiva* is hypokeimenon of all manifestation, and he has a multitude of states, or forms. There is nothing in the Universe, as it is reflected in the mind, that is not *śiva*, the same way there is nothing in nature that is not a form of energy.

Of many states of *śiva*, there is a special, distinguished state that is called the state of *bhairava*. It is an undifferentiated, unvaried condition, or form, that lacks any particulars, but is full of all potentialities. The state of *bhairava* is like the stillness and tranquility of homogeneous air. This analogy with air will be developed further.

One of the inherent characteristics of air is the presence of ever appearing and dissolving fluctuations of pressure, temperature, and density. Similarly, there is the primordial everpresent throbbing of fluctuations in *śiva*. This throbbing is called *spanda*.

When fluctuations of pressure occur in still air, they might dissipate without any manifested phenomena, or they might give birth to wind or whirls. The same way, *spanda* might give rise to a more differentiated state of *śiva*. The energy of fluctuations in the state of *bhairava* is called *bhairavī*, or *parāśakti*, or ultimate potentiality.

When this energy of pressure fluctuations transforms into wind or whirls, then the air becomes manifestly non-uniform, or differentiated. These differentiations might become sounds, lenses causing visual distortions, twisters, etc. Similarly, *parāśakti* might give rise to specific potentialities, or energies, that cause sensory perception, speech, thoughts, emotions, etc.

A specific form of the *parāśakti* might be of *parā-aparā* type, or of *aparā* type, and is called N-*śakti*, where N denotes a particular experience or manifestation or process.

---

[57] *śaktiś ca nāma bhāvasya svaṃ rūpaṃ mātṛkalpitam* TA.1.69.a

The *parā-aparā* type of *śakti* is potentiality, born of differentiations, caused by *parāśakti*. *Parā-aparā* can directly dissolve into *parāśakti*. The differentiations caused by it could dissolve or evolve into a self-perpetuating cycle of arising, relative stability and cessation. In the last case *parā-aparā-śakti* becomes a multitude of *aparā-śakti*-s.

The *aparā* type of *śakti* is the potentiality born of differentiations, caused by *parā-aparāśakti*. Like turbulence in the air, in which the disappearance of one whirl causes new disturbances in the flow of air, so are differentiations and manifestations born of *aparā* type of *śakti*. Cessation of one phenomenon gives birth to others. The perpetuation of arising, relative stability and of cessation of phenomena is called *saṃsāra*. Abiding in the state of *bhairava* is the cessation of *samsāra*, or *nirvana*.

The state of *bhairava*, in which the energy of fluctuations is at the threshold of causing some phenomena, is called *prabhu*.

cicchakti the ability to illuminate, to attend to.[58]

ānandaśakti the ability to experience bliss;
śiva's freedom of will.[59]

icchāśakti astonishment, surprise at one's own freedom of will.[60]

Gaining freedom is manifested through astonishment. Flight from freedom is the flight towards the certain, controllable, and predictable.

jñānaśakti the ability to have direct experience (lit. "to touch").[61]

kriyāśakti the ability to be related or connected in any way.[62]

tattva an attribute, a quality of mental "things" (ideas, percepts, gestalts, volitions, emotions, feelings, actions, speech, and anything that might be an object of introspection);
that which patterns fragmentation, breaks whole into parts, but by doing so, provides for comparability between distinct entities, or particulars (*svalakṣana*-s);
type of dynamic in *prakāśa*.

---

58 ... *prakāśarūpatā cicchaktiḥ* AbhTs.1.5
59 ... *tasya ca svātantryamānandaśaktiḥ* AbhTs.1.5
60 ... *taccamatkāra icchāśaktiḥ*... AbhTs.1.5
61 ... *āmarśātmakatā jñānaśaktiḥ*... AbhTs.1.5
62 *sarvākārayogitvaṃ kriyāśaktiḥ* AbhTs.1.5

> A *tattva* may be compounded with several other *tattva*-s, it might have another *tattva* as a component, and it might be perceptible under some circumstances.
>
> An important aspect of all *tattva*-s, other than *śivatattva*, is that there are three modes of expression:
>
> being absent;
>
> being present in some degree, but amenable to vanishing, or dissolution;
>
> being present in some degree, but rigidly split away from vanishing.

The practical goal of *Pratyabhijñā* is to reconfigure one's own mental processes to get rid of those *tattva* expressions that are rigidly split from vanishing.

According to Trika, there are 36 fundamental *tattva*-s:

śiva-tattva

śakti-tattva

sadāśiva-tattva

īśvara-tattva

śuddhavidyā-tattva

māyā-tattva

kalā-tattva

vidyā-tattva

rāga-tattva

kāla-tattva

niyati-tattva

puruṣa-tattva

prakṛti-tattva

buddhi-tattva

ahaṃkāra-tattva

manas-tattva

five *karmendriya*-s

five *jñānedriya*-s

five *tanmātra*-s

five *mahābhūta*-s.

They are defined below.

Each *tattva* is sustained and supported by the *tattva*-s above it. The topmost, *śivatattva*, is therefore called *anāśrita*, that is, "not supported."

Various degrees of their expression cause the multitude of personal experiences and states of mind. Analysis of experiences and states using *tattva*-s as dimensions, or categories, is integral to the path of the *Pratyabhijñā* system. Similarly to the way experiences are analysed in Buddhism with the schema of dependent co-arising, all "mental" phenomena are analyzed in *Pratyabhijñā* as a configuration of *tattva*-s.

Although there is a strong similarity between the lowest 25 *tattva*-s and the *tattva*-s of the *Saṃkhya* system, there is no equivalency between them.

śivatattva the most abstract attribute of what is to be perceived or experienced or felt or performed — being self-illuminating;[63]
that which appears as the illumination (*prakāśa*);[64]
transition between presence of some mental "things" and the complete absence of any mental "things" (this is not a transition having any duration, since the diminution (preceding the complete absence) or the growth (right after appearance) are not parts of this transition);
fading of any activated mental "thing" into emptiness, void of all mental "things;"
subtle vibration that starts manifestation of any mental "thing";
emptiness – fullness continuum as an attribute of mental "things."[65]

It is the ultimate basis of all other *tattva*-s.[66]

This *tattva* is the substratum of all manifestation — for the emptiness is the universal transition point. Therefore, *śivatattva* is the ultimate instrument of liberation.

---

[63] *jñeyasya hi paraṃ tattvaṃ yaḥ prakāśātmakaḥ śivaḥ* TA.1.52.a
[64] *yad etat prakāśarūpaṃ śivatattvamuktam* AbhTs.3.1
[65] *anāśritaḥ śūnyamātā...* TA.6.43b
[66] *yadetatsvaprakāśaṃsarvatattvāntarbhūtaṃparaṃtattvamuktaṃ* AbhTs.5.4

śaktitattva transition from one form into another (as opposed to the transition between a form and the void, which is the *śivatattva*);
pure dynamic, devoid of any substratum;
subtle self-reflection of *śiva* prior to manifestation.[67]

sadāśivatattva "I"-disposition of thought;
transition inwards (the same way a visual image of a jar perceived by the eyes for several minutes, moves into the internal plane when the eyes are closed, instead of simply disappearing);[68]
determination of the degree of correspondence of appearances to a sense, a knowledge, or a meaning of those appearances.[69]

īśvaratattva "That"-disposition of thought;
transition outwards (the same way an imagined jar moves into the external plane when the eyes are opened and see the same jar).

A yet-to-be-externalized intention initially manifests itself in the subtle body by influencing flows of *prāṇa*, *apāna*, etc. — this influence is mediated by *īśvaratattva*.[70]

śuddhavidyātattva co-referentiality between "I"-disposition and "That"-disposition of thought. This co-referentiality makes any action indifferent with respect to "I"–"That" dispositions.[71]

Sadāśivatattva is a projection of *śakti* onto the domain of perception; *īśvaratattva* is a projection of *śakti* onto the domain of actions; *śuddhavidyātattva* is a projection of *śakti* onto the domain of desires, for it is a desire that correlates the internal and the external planes.

In the absence of *tattva*-s other than *śivatattva*, *śaktitattva*, *sadāśivatattva*, *īśvaratattva* and *śuddhavidyātattva*, which state is called *pati* ("being the master"), knowledge and perception are not quite differentiated from action. In this state, knowledge and perception are both the agent and the instrument of action. In it,

[67] *parabhāvāt tu tatsūkṣmaṃ śaktitattvaṃ nigadyate* TA.13.191.b
[68] *īśvaro bahirunmeṣo nimeṣo'ntaḥ sadāśivaḥ* IPK 3.1.3.a
[69] ... *buddhimātā sadāśivaḥ* TA.6.43b
[70] *īśvaraḥ prāṇamātā ca vidyā dehapramātṛtā* TA.6.44.a
[71] *sāmānādhikaraṇyaṃ ca sadvidyāhamidaṃdhiyoḥ* IPK 3.1.3.b

the initial impulse[72] that leads to the expression of *śivatattva* and *śaktitattva* has not yet caused two dispositions, "I" and "That," to form a duality such that a transition from "I" to "That" and from "That" to "I" is no longer spontaneous and unimpeded.

The following three terms — *māyā*, *māyāśakti* and *māyātattva* — though closely related, are not indentical. The same could be said about other *tattva*-s, since it is a frequent source of confusion: N-*śakti*, N-*tattva* and N are not necessarily denoting the same concept. As a rule, N-*śakti* is a potentiality and N-*tattva* an actuality; both are connected with the phenomenon denoted with N.

māyā — the lack of clear perception of the presence of the *tattva*-s, starting with *kalā* and ending with *pṛthvī* (see below);[73]
whatever is possessing of resistance, opposition to transitions — that is, an expression of *māyā*.[74]

Māyā avoids being manifested by constant incitement of *kalā*-s. The incitement is caused by selective masking of conditions that determine the relevancy of *kalā*-s activation, thus leaving dominant only desire/action aspects. Because of the consequences of this incitement, *māyā* is called bewildering.[75]

She is behind the tendency of ego to expand itself.

māyāśakti — the potency to obscure, to conceal in a degree that leads one to take the illusory for the real (in the relative, not the absolute, sense of the illusory–real dichotomy).

māyātattva — inhibition or masking of the augmentation of *tattva*-s, listed below *māyātattva*. *māyātattva* conceals the fact and the process of fragmentation and the patterns of the fragmentation by all 30 *tattva*-s listed below it. Indirectly, it thus masks its own presence.

The power of knowledge and correct analysis are capable of inferring the presence of *māyātattva*, despite all this masking.

The following five *tattva*-s, beginning with *kalātattva* and ending with *niyatitattva*, are collectively referred to as *kañcuka*-s (or

[72] It is an expression of *vimarśa*.
[73] *kalādīnāṃ tattvānām avivekomāyā* ShS.III.3
[74] *bhāvānāṃ yatpratīghāti vapur māyātmakaṃ hi tat* TA 3.10.a
[75] *māyā vimohinī nāma kalāyāḥ kalanaṃ sthitam* VBh.95.a

armors of an individual). Their common property is to strengthen with time and to become more and more rigid.[76]

kalātattva transfer of the energy of will onto the field of habitual, impulsive or automatized actions;
automaticity of action, skill.

The presence of *kalātattva* provides for virtuoso performance in all arts, but because of the automaticity, it limits to some degree the creativity of the performer. It also provides for obsessive and impulsive behaviours like playing videogames or Internet browsing.

The power of *kalātattva* to shape consciousness is so strong and universal among humans that it is said by *Bṛhaspati* (quoted in TA.9.208b) to be like a second *citi*. Consciousness, shaped only by *śivatattva*, *śaktitattva*, *sadāśivatattva*, *īśvaratattva* and *śuddhavidyātattva*, has no definite form; it is like the Heraclitean river, which stays the same despite the flows of water being never the same. *Kalātattva* changes that indefiniteness — as if adding polished facets to a natural ruby.

The impluse, the incitement behind the *kalātattva* is *māyā*. This is so, because in the inner world only consistent and automatic concealment is effective. *Karma* expresses itself through *kalātattva* (but not only through it).

vidyātattva transfer of the energy of will onto the field of meanings, abstractions, and scripts of actions;
that which marks what is pleasurable, what is suffering, and what is neither, separately and in addition to the instinct; that which relates any knowledge to the needs of the corporeal body and of the material existence;
pramātṛ of stimulation coming from the corporeal body (that is, from internal organs, from muscles, from joints); that which integrates proprioceptive signals into perception.

In general, *vidyātattva* operates on meta-levels, being an instrument of actions upon *buddhi*; that is, it is not

[76] See R.Torella, "The *kañcuka*-s in the *śaiva* and *vaiṣṇava* Tantric Tradition: A Few Considerations between Theology and Grammar." In *Studies in Hinduism II*, edited by G. Oberhammer, 55-86, 1998.

being augmented onto *grāhya* directly.[77] *Vidyātattva* primes perception, action, or desire to conform to general categories.

For example, a percept of fire augmented with *vidyātattva* might acquire qualities like "warmth" or "burning," even if the subject of perception if too far from the fire to feel either warmth or burning. Another example is given by composing a sentence to comply with a particular grammatical structure, grammar being a meta-level of ordinary language.

Though quite limited in purpose, *vidyātattva*, being a realization of *vidyāśakti*, facilitates counteracting *māyā*.[78]

rāgatattva transfer of the energy of will into nurturing an attachment;
an attribute that provides for a subtle restoration of desire (potentially directed towards a new object) even after the desire was completely satisfied;[79] intense affection that is not specific, that is without a definite object.[80]

Rāgatattva prevents positive or negative emotions from becoming just memories. It is more like a resolve to keep these emotions relevant to one's self.

Whether some experience would be positive or negative from the point of view of feelings depends in part on physiology. But whether *rāgatattva* is attached to the experience or not is more a result of one's own intentions.

Sometimes one can observe how *rāgatattva* is affixed to some positive or negative experiences when the experiences are recollected. This augmentation might be accompanied by thoughts like "I will pursue this" or "I really like that" or "This is important for me," etc.

[77] *tattvaṃ vidyākhyamasṛjatkaraṇaṃ paramātnamaḥ MrA*
[78] *tasyaiśvaryasvabhāvasya paśubhāve prakāśikā* |
vidyāśaktiḥ tirodhānakarī māyābhidhā punaḥ || IPK.3.1.7
[79] *rāgatattvamiti proktaṃ yattatraivoparañjakam* |
na cāvairāgyamātraṃ tattatrāpy āsaktivṛttitaḥ || TA.9.200
viraktāv api tṛptasya sūkṣmarāgavyavasthiteḥ | TA.9.201a
[80] *rāgo'bhiṣvaṅgātmā viṣayacchedaṃ vinaiva sāmānyaḥ* TtP.48.ab

Whatever inner construct was created with intention, the support for its existence might by removed by unintending. After the support is removed, the flux of things will gradually dissolve it. Here is a practice that could be done with respect to this *tattva*: wherever you detect a manifestation of the *rāgatattva*, recollect the moment it was affixed to a positive or negative experience. Then, without attempting to change the feeling about the experience, retract the resolve to maintain its relevance to yourself, beyond what is dictated by reason. What is dictated by reason can be clearly understood after *rāgatattva* is dissolved.

Rāgatattva is that which creates *upādāna*[81] in the Buddhist schema of dependent co-arising.

kālatattva in the domain of perception and knowledge, it is an attribute of duration, the quality of having a location in time, the mark of being "before/after" some event;
in the domain of actions, sense of pace (that which enables one to sing in sync with music or to mirror synchronously actions of another);
in the domain of desires, it is the duration of postponement of gratification, beyond which a lack of satisfaction causes distress, anxiety, etc. or timing of some events (like when one resolves "I will wake up at exactly at 7:40 am" and does wake up at that time).

niyatitattva strong inclination towards a particular way of acting, thinking, or feeling;
kalā, devoid of the strength of immediacy;
transition between apparent cause and apparent effect (*niyatitattva* is the link between *karma* and the consequences of it);
in the domain of perception and knowledge, it is the bias of a syllogism, especially of logical fallacies;
in the domain of actions, it is a habitual coordination of muscular activity (for example, stepping on an unmoving escalator, that was moving in the past, creates muscular activation inadequate to the situation);
in the domain of desires/will, it is the absoluteness of

[81] See discussion to Sutra 8.

acceptance/rejection (like "this is intolerable"; "that is the best thing ever"; "I never can do that," etc.).

Whatever is possessing *niyatitattva*, acquires an appearance of "necessity."

kañcuka an armor of an individual;
one the five *tattva*-s: *kalā-tattva*, *vidyā-tattva*, *rāga-tattva*, *kāla-tattva*, and *niyati-tattva*.

The presence of *kañcuka*-s is revealed by the following persistent and pervasive phenomena:

preservation of "I" is a habit; that is, a set of skills invoked almost instinctively, personal speech being the primary example;

knowledge is dedicated to survival, either personal or of some substitute (like family, tribe, social group, philosophical system, scientific theory, etc.); the validity of knowledge is derived from authority; asking for opinions of an authority is the origin of knowledge;

relishing the very desire for "I" to be;

a resolve that an absence of "I" expression should last no longer than some preset period of time (that might vary with circumstances);

the conviction that it is *necessary* for "I" to be.

There might be other expressions. Any aspect of one's individuality might have several armors.

A very important practice with regard to the *kañcuka*-s is deconstruction of long-term, persistent expressions of them in one's own behaviour. By conscious removal of actual expressions of these five *tattva*-s, an "individual," devoid of armors, would be eventually dissolved by the flux of things.

The point of the practice is not to get killed, or to die from exposure, or to become a mindless cult follower of some strong willed individual or group, but to get rid of irrational rigidity and to understand how the armors and the very idea of unchangable and sharply bounded "individual" contribute to self-perpetuating unhappiness, stress, and pain.

puruṣatattva transfer of the energy of will into *prakṛtitattva* and *tattva*-s listed below it;
attachment to being necessarily defined in terms of *tattva*-s listed below *prakṛtitattva*, or as an overall limited individual.

When *puruṣatattva* is present but all *tattva*-s listed below it are registering void, it is a state, which is sometimes called *śūnya*.

prakṛtitattva the delflection of the power of will into the ruts of biological programs;
the quality of "non-sentience";
the quality of being "external," "material," "non-mental,"

prakṛtitattva has three pervasive distinct characteristics: *sattva*, *rajas*, and *tamas*.

In the domain of perception/knowledge:
rajas manifests itself as adaptation of percepts, memory, notions to the current flow of stimulation; it projects difference and contrast;
tamas – as inertia of percepts, memory, notions, etc., that allows to project identity between unique perceptual instances and to form abstractions;
sattva – as an expansion of perceptual field and formation of new percepts, notions, images, ideas, etc.

For additional details, see *buddhi*.

In the domain of actions:
rajas manifests itself as the dynamic of waves of *prāṇa*, *apāna*, etc.;
tamas – as long-term potentiation of physiological activities;
sattva – as relaxation.

in the domain of desires:
rajas manifests itself as passion and attachment to action;
tamas – as attachment to delusions and persistence of will;
sattva – as attachment to happiness, comfort, and knowledge.

buddhitattva the transfer of the energy of will into the domain of knowledge (see *buddhi*), which enables reasoning, men-

tal gestures (*mati*), and the control (through definiteness, precision and robustness of knowledge) of perception, desires, and actions;
that which makes *buddhi* active.

ahaṃkāratattva in the domain of perception and knowledge, it is the attribute of "mine–not–mine";
in the domain of actions, it is "becoming someone," or identification of "I" with something limited and well defined, or self-expression;
in the domain of desires/will, it is the "antagonistic-sympathetic to me" dimension of feelings.

ahaṃkāratattva inherits from *buddhitattva* three flavors — *sattva*, *rajas* and *tamas*.[82]

manastattva the transfer of the energy of will into the domain self-reflection, introspection;
an attribute that makes mental "things" subject to comparison, to memory recall, to association, and to all conscious mental operations in general; that which makes *manas* active.

Manastattva is instrumental in separation of "mental" things into conscious and subconscious, while *māyātattva* is instrumental in separation of the unconscious.

karmendriya ideo-motoric quality: any construct, possessing it, upon being illuminated by *prakāśa*, produces actual muscular or physiological activity.

There are five general categories, resulting in activities responsible for speech, movements of hands and fingers, locomotion, excretion, and sexual manifestations; there are many others like those responsible for movements of eyes or changes of body temperature.

jñānendriya these attributes encompass all perceptual features provided by sense organs: colors, pitch of sound, temperature, loudness, etc.
There are five types of *jñānendriya*-s provided by the faculties of vision, hearing, taste, smell and by the somatosensory system.

---

[82] *buddhitattvādahaṃkāraḥ punarjātastridhā priye* |
sāttvikorājasaścaiva tāmasaśca prakīrtitaḥ || SvaT.11.75

buddhīndriya = *jñānendriya*

tanmātra modality of perception; a smell, a taste, a touch, a sound, a visual image — as such, in general.[83]

Because of the presence of *tanmātra* one can tell if a sensation is a sound, a taste, etc. Weakening of the influence of these *tattva*-s causes synesthesia (for example, perceiving colors of musical notes) or integrating features from different modalities as to make them comparable.

A component of many practices of this system is the process of recollecting experiences in as many perceptual details as possible. It helps to recollect a particular experience as projected onto different modalities. How was it, if restricted only to visual image, or only to sounds, or to the non-verbal components of speech? How might it be described by using only smells, or tastes, or sense of touch?

The modality of smell is connected with the inner self on a deep level. Heraclitus once noticed that

> Thus in the abysmal dark
> the soul is known by scent.

puryaṣṭaka the doors, or channels, of perception, of which there are eight: the five *tanmātra*-s and the three components of the *antaḥkaraṇa*.

mahābhūta-s these represent types of ideas, or patterns of dividing stream of stimulation into entities:
pṛthivī type indicates an idea of something fixed, like a solid body — not subject to change due to the context, neither in substance nor in form;
jala type indicates an idea of something like a fluid, of something that has an invariant substance, but a form completely dependent on the environment;
tejas type indicates an idea of something like the light, of intensity, energy, an idea of something having no definite form, but adopting attributes of the environment;
vāyu indicates an idea of something like air, all-pervading; of something having no manifested substance or form,

[83] *yatsāmānyaṃ hi gandhatvaṃ gandhatanmātranāma tat* TA.9.281.a

but the presence of which is inferred from manifested elements;
ākāśa indicates an idea that stands for absence of something else, an idea of the void.

All of these types can be illustrated with a favorite object of Indian philosophical discourse — a jar. The jar as a solid body is an example of *pṛthivī*. The water in the jar is an example of *jala*. The round and hollow shape of the jar is conveyed by light gradients, which exemplify *tejas*. The usability of the jar for cooking, not just for holding water, is an example of *vāyu*. And an abstraction of a jar, as a rigid shape devoid of space and time particularizations — the empty space within — is an example of *ākāśa*.

Another illustration of *mahābhūta*-s is afforded by a Japanese garden: *pṛthivī* are the stones, *jala* is the flow of water shaped by the stones; *tejas* is the light that integrates elements of the garden into a landscape; *vāyu* is *fuzei*, or that breeze of feelings evoked by the experience of being in the garden, which cannot easily be attributed to any particular component; *ākāśa* is the contrasting void left after exiting the garden, when the enchantment of *fuzei* is dispersed by the flood of city irritants.

One of the important applications of the concept of *mahābhūta*-s to the analysis of psychological processes is the analysis of ideas of "self." Ego attempts to present the "self" as an unchangable, sharply bounded entity — by projecting *pṛthivī* attribute onto it. The *pṛthivī-tattva*, being the last in the sequence of *tattva*-s, partakes in and is supported by all *tattva*-s. Thus, is it pervasive, robust, and very difficult to dissolve. The weakening of *pṛthivī-tattva*, that affords local dissolution of it in every context, is called in Buddhism "stream-entry."

If that attempt of Ego fails, the next presentation is using *jala* as the pattern, etc. In reality, in different contexts, the "self" might have different patterns. One of the fundamental ideas of Buddha is that of *anātman* — all of these patterns are projected onto "self" and are not inherent in it.

This ends the description of the 36 *tattva*-s.

saṃskāra	latent mental impression that synthesizes direct perceptions with feelings, opinions, actions, and volitions; a synergetic composite of five consecutive *tattva*-s — from *kalātattva* to *niyatitattva* — with perceptual impressions. *Saṃskāra* is a mold for future fruits of *karma*.
śarīra	the totality of proprioceptive signals; all stimulation from internal organs and muscles.
citta	a stable mental complex (*skandha*) that consists of interconnected impressions, actions and feelings. Such a complex perpetuates itself by mutual activations between the components. Cascading activations and mutations of *citta*'s components are called *vṛtti* (sometimes perceived as a "train of thought"). As there are many such complexes, because of their schematic nature, they tend to coalesce with time into loosely connected large nets. A primary example of such a net is the faculty of speech. Nodes of this net correspond to "clouds" of semantic, phonetic, and representational features, and articulation sequences of particular words. Here is an example of cascading activations: Silent articulation of the word "jar" might cause activation of the memory of a jar used as an object of contemplation. The recalled image of the jar might, in turn, lead to activation of the memory of tasty food that was prepared in that very jar yesterday. The idea of food, in turn, brings forward the realizaion that one is hungry now. The feeling of hunger reminds one that there is no grain left to cook. That means that one has to find some cash to go to the market. And so on. Such a net is referred to as "Indra's net of illusions."[84] Attaining *citta-vṛtti-nirodha* — the cessation or confinement of cascading activations and mutations of the components of a *citta* is defined as the goal of yoga practices in YS.I.2.[85] In the *Pratyabhijñā* system this goal

[84] *indrajālamayaṃ viśvaṃ vyastaṃ* VBh.102.a
[85] *yogaścittavṛttinirodhaḥ*

is achieved through re-identification, or recognition, of one's own nature as that of *śiva*. The cause of the cessation of *citta-vṛtti*-s is the dissolution of complexes of *tattva*-s that were deflecting the impulse of the inherent free will (*vimarśa*) into activation of the components of *citta*.

Sometimes the whole of the nets of mental complexes is called *citta*, and in that case it is used in the meaning "ordinary mind."

saṃsāra being carried away by the appearances deemed external;
limitation of free will by the dynamic net of perceptual illusions (*māyā*);
virtual worlds one builds for oneself and plays a role in.

Saṃsāra has several scales. One is of seconds — it is the processes of perception, cognition, and action. A bigger one is that of hours — it is the processes of changes from sleep to wakefulness, from tension to relaxation, from activity to rest, etc. An even bigger one is that of days and months — it is the processes of seasonal/monthly physiological changes in the body/mind. Bigger yet is that of years — it is the processes of personal changes during a lifetime, like childhood, adolescence, adulthood, etc.

saṃsārin he, who abides in *saṃsāra*;
one who is totally immersed into virtual worlds of mundane existence.

mala is a persistent construct of a special kind that masks, inhibits, or outweighs other potentially active structures. It is called *mala* (lit. "impurity") because it is causing faults.

Three types of *mala*-s are defined in *Pratyabhijñā*: *āṇavamala*, *māyīyamala* and *kārmamala*. Behind all types of *mala*-s is the *māyāśakti*.[86]

The *āṇavamala*, being an evolute of *icchāśakti*, has the nature of willful self-restriction.

[86] ... *māyāśaktyaiva tattrayam* IPK.3.2.5.b

As stated in the commentary to *sūtra* 9, *icchāśakti*, manifesting as an unobstructed self-will, when abridged and virtualized, turns into *āṇavamala*, *āṇavamala*, manifesting itself as the sense of otherness and the lack of self-sufficiency.[87]

An *āṇavamala* manifests itself as a strong bias towards well defined borders between concepts of "I" and "Not-Me". These borders are created by activation of aversions, preferences, and affections. An *āṇavamala* is not, per se, a preference of one alternative over another, but rather a *relish* of such preference. When such relish is augmented by *rāgatattva*, it turns into an addiction to imposing such preferences.

The relinquishment of the freedom of will while fully aware and the lack of full awareness while following one's own will — this is the twofold *āṇavamala*. It is twofold in ways it impairs one's true character.[88]

When *āṇavamala* is present, logic is seen as devoid of a reflection of self and, thus, knowledge bears that emptiness which is as if devoid of "self." So, *kārmamala* tends to be illogical, or even irrational, because of the resolve to manifest the fullness-of-self in opposition to pure and full awareness.

A sense of powerlessness, or lack of freedom when a logical and consistent schema of a situation sinks in, comes from a forceful assertion of one's own prior resolutions which, by virtue of being addicted to (that is, augmented with *rāgatattva*), come into contradiction with the reality ("reality" is defined here as the part of perceptual space, which is most independent of the tides of desires).

The *āṇavamala* is the root cause of two other types of *mala*-s.

The *māyīyamala* is a fragmentation of experiencing that inhibits the expression of the freedom of will and restricts the freedom to act.

[87] *apratihatasvātantryarūpā icchāśaktiḥ saṃkucitāsatī apūrṇamanyatārūpamāṇavaṃmalam*

[88] *svātantryahānir bodhasya svātantryasyāpy abodhatā |*
dvidhāṇavaṃ malam idaṃ svasvarūpāpahānitaḥ || IPK.3.2.4

As stated in the commentary to the 9-th *sūtra*, *jñāna śaktiḥ*, at reaching the state of directly experiencing something particular, gradually, beginning with contraction, and moving towards delimitation of the ablility to experience everything, that is there to be experienced, having been in the configurations of *buddhīndriya*-s and *antaḥkaraṇa* through locking into excessive abbreviation, becomes *māyīyamala*, manifesting itself as a flow [of attention bias] into mere fragments of what is there to be experienced.[89]

One of the strongest expressions of the *māyīyamala* is the assumption of the spoken words to be true and thus, when uttered by a figure one considers an authority or an apriory trusted source, making them a guide for further actions and/or the analysis of a situation. To counter the effects of *māyīyamala*, a functional assumption of inherent indefiniteness of any perception is of great help (as done by philosophers, adhering to skepticism, or by poker players reading facial expressions).

The *kārmamala* constrains an action to a script laced with personal preferences that impairs awareness.

As stated in the commentary to the 9-th *sūtra*, *kriyāśakti* at reaching the state of performing some definite action, constraining in stages the unlimited creativity and having assumed the configuration of *karmendriya*-s through locking into excessive abbreviation, arriving at an excessively encapsulated condition [becomes] *kārmamala*, consisting in acting in conformity with expedient–ineffective [axis].[90]

Action, in its activation and structure, might be affected by other actions, by desires, by perceptions of inner and outer stimuli and by knowledge. *kārmamala* is a restriction of such influences to actions and desires only. Just before an action is activated, the perceptive attention is inhibited, or masked, allowing only other

[89] *jñānaśaktiḥ krameṇasaṃkocādbhede sarvajñatvasya kiṃcijjñatvāpteḥ antaḥkaraṇabuddhīndriyatāpattipūrvamatyantasaṃkocagrahaṇena bhinnavedyaprathārūpaṃ māyīyaṃ malam*

[90] *kriyāśaktiḥ krameṇa bhede sarvakartṛtvasya kiṃcitkartṛtvāpteḥ karmendriyarūpasaṃkocagrahaṇapūrvaṃ atyantaparimitatāṃ prāptā śubhāśubhānuṣṭhānamayaṃ kārmaṃ malam*

actions and desires to shape the current action, and making one as if momentarily blind.

dhyāna meditation. It is defined thus in YS.3.2.[91] and in VBh.146.a.[92]

It is a state of *buddhi* in the context of strong concentration of attention in which *buddhi*:

a. is steady, invariable, unchangeable;

b. has a single concept, or knowledge, that is not supported or conditioned by anything else present in short-term memory (that is, not conditioned by other concepts, by a percept, by an idea, by action, by wish, by desire, etc.);

c. directs attention of the senses, *manas*, and *ahaṃkāra* onto one object only; this concentration of attention does not result in less awareness;[93]

d. makes the flow of stimuli coalesce with that one object (*ekatānatā*).

For practical techniques of meditation, see [Ram98].

Meditation is not contemplation. During meditation there is no arrangement of thoughts; there is no intention to get somewhere, or to find a solution or an answer.

Hypnotic trance is related to meditation but is in many ways opposite to it. A big difference between the two is in reactivity to speech. In hypnotic trance, speech is automatically relevant to one's self, and some speech attains the power of an imperative. In meditation, speech is just a sound that has no immediate meaning or power to control. It passes through as if one is no different from the surrounding air — without resistance and without attraction to it.

[91] *tatra pratyayaikatānatā dhyānam*

[92] *dhyānaṃ hi niścalā buddhirnirākārā nirāśrayā*

[93] The degree of awareness might be known after the meditation by the degree one is able to recollect everything that was going on at the time of the meditation.

Another big difference is that the scope of awareness during hypnosis becomes narrow and focused, while in meditation it becomes broader and indefinite.

Yet another difference is in the direction and intensity of predominant flows of *vāyu*-s. During both states the flows are primarily through *iḍā* and *piṅgalā*. In meditation, the controlling flows are from *viśuddha cakra* downwards, while in hypnosis, the controlling flows are from *mūladhāra* upwards. In meditation, the flows are less intense than in the hypnotic state.

samādhi the state of absorption that is defined thus in YS.3.3: That same *dhyāna*, when the object, that attention is directed to, is as if devoid of it's own substance or of unchangable characteristics, is *samādhi*.[94]

The definition of *samādhi*, given in verses 6,7, and 8 of HYP.4, is on three planes: the gross, the subtle and the ultimate, correspondingly.

As salt dissolves in the waters of the sea without a trace, so a homologous unity between the breath and *manas* is realized as *samādhi*.[95]

When *prāṇa* is depleted and all fabrications by *manas* dissolve, then the self-sameness of the sentiment is realized as *samādhi*.[96]

The identity between the [limited] individual and the ultimate "Self" [that has assumed that limited configuration, which is perceived as an individual], the equality between the two — the state in which all notions, formed in the mind due to volition, vanish — is realized as *samādhi*.[97]

vyutthāna the state of consciousness that is characterized by the presence of duality subject/object of perception, though the duality is rendered ineffective in comparison

[94] *tadevārthamātranirbhāsaṃ svarūpaśūnyamiva samādhiḥ*

[95] *salile saindhavaṃ yadvatsāmyaṃ bhajati yogataḥ* |
tathātmamanasorikyaṃ samādhirabhidhīyate || HYP.4.5

[96] *yadā saṃkṣīyate prāṇo mānasaṃ ca pralīyate* |
tadā samarasatvaṃ ca samādhirabhidhīyate ||

[97] *tatsamaṃ ca dvayoraikyaṃ jīvātmaparamātmanoḥ* |
praṇaṣṭasarvasaṅkalpaḥ samādhiḥ so'bhidhīyate ||

with "ordinary" consciousness. The strength of this duality, originating with *āṇavamala*, might be diminished to such a degree that entry into *samādhi* is attained intermittently with little effort. The transition between *samādhi* and the "ordinary" state of consciousness is an example of *vyutthāna*. As said in *Śivasūtravārtika*, *vyutthāna* appears as an allayed disunion.[98]

nimitta a pointer to a percept or mental construct that is the object of absorption, resulting from *dhyāna*.

mantra a formula consisting of phonemes and silence, and characterized by a particular articulation. *Mantra* shapes thinking and primes psycho-physiological processes. It might have a literal meaning, but it is not required. A *mantra* practice is a paradoxical way of directing the faculty of speech at transcending the duality "I"–"That," in the arising of which that same faculty is instrumental.

[98] *vyutthānaṃ ca bhavecchāntabhedābhāsamitīryate* ShSVR 1.5:8

Postulates and commentaries to them

Though the core text of *Pratyabhijñāhṛdayam* consists of only twenty sentences, the connection between them is not self-evident. Here is an outline.

1, 2	The paradigm.
3–7	How manifoldness of phenomena arises, how *māyā* comes to be.
8	Expressiveness of the paradigm.
9	Arising of *samsāra*.
10, 11	The five acts.
12, 13	Liberation as a consequence of the awareness of the five acts.
14–20	Technical aspects of the process of liberation.

चितिः स्वतन्त्रा विश्वसिद्धिहेतुः ॥ १॥

citiḥ svatantrā viśvasiddhihetuḥ || *1* ||

Citi, possessing of free will, is the cause of the efficiency of everything mental (ideas, concepts, percepts, gestalts, volitions, emotions, feelings, actions, speech, etc. and anything that might be an object of introspection).

In particular, *citi* is the cause of the attainment of ultimate liberation.

This first postulate gives the organizing principle that brings a dynamic aspect into conglomerates of the 36 *tattva*-s — *citi*. Any model of psychological processes that would be constructed in this system will have expressions of *citi*, potentially on multiple time scales, as the primary impulse. *Citi* posesses both free will and the ablity for long-term potentiation, to make expressions of free will lasting.

Given the assumption of the existence of free will, a naïve answer to the question "Who or what posesses free will?" is "Me". As strange as it sounds, this answer is wrong. Ordinarily, "me" refers to the Ego. But the Ego is nothing more than a wave attempting to freeze in the ocean of *cit*. It is important to realize that free will is in the very fabric of consciousness — it is *not localized* in the Ego.

Cit cannot be referred to as "I" or "me" or "it" or "that" or "this" without committing an error, since all these words, if used in the ordinary sense, cast a duality[99] onto that which is ultimately singular.

Ego should not be thought of as something definitely bad. A strong ego is a prerequisite for the knowledge of Self and, thus, it is a prerequisite to treading the path to enlightenment. On the other hand, a strong ego is a big hurdle on this path, since it limits one's view, actions, and expressions of free will. As Swami Rama put it,[100]

> The emergence of the ego as a small island upon which to stand is an important step in the evolution of self-consciousness. The ego enables one to be conscious of

[99]that is, they are *vikalpa*-s
[100][Ram82]

> oneself, though the self that one is conscious of is extremely circumscribed.

This *sūtra* states that *citi* is the cause of the efficiency of everything mental. It follows that each mental obstacle, distraction, fault, and each mental perfection, attainment, and realization — all have substantially the same cause, that might have different configurations. Direct experience with the transmutation of mental constructs will make this statement more comprehensible.

The injunction of this *sūtra* is to search for ultimate causes within.

There is a *double entendre* in this *sūtra*: *Citi, being the instrument of her own expansion, is the cause of the efficiency of the intellectual faculty to make everything a subject of perception and cognition.*

स्वेच्छया स्वभित्तौ विश्वमुन्मीलयति ॥ २॥

svecchayā svabhittau viśvam unmīlayati || 2||

During self-fragmentation, *citi*, of her own free will, causes the Universe to be manifested on herself as on a screen.

"Self-fragmentation" here means "self-variation" of a mirror reflecting an object. The reflection in the mirror appears to have parts, fragments, boundaries, etc. But unlike a material object, like a jar, the reflection is infinitely elastic, being easily morphed into reflection of another object.[101]

Citi is like a reflection in a mirror: whatever forms or configurations she assumes, she retains infinite plasticity. In addition, she herself is the will to change. Practices of *Pratyabhijñāhṛdayam* system are based on the assumption of both self-will and plasticity.

[101] *nirmale makure yadvadbhānti bhūmijalādayaḥ* TA.3.4.a

तन्नाना अनुरूपग्राह्यग्राहकभेदात् ॥ ३॥

tannānā anurūpagrāhyagrāhakabhedāt || 3||

The Universe is so at variance with itself (meaning that there are distinct planes of perception and that the same thing is perceived as different from itself under different circumstances or in different contexts) because of divergences between *grāhaka* and correpond-ing to it (or conformable to it) *grāhya*.

The first question any monistic system, like *Pratyabhijñāhṛdayam*, has to answer is, What is the source of the apparent variety and manifoldness of the Universe?

Here is the answer. In the process of perception and cognition that produces this sense of difference or manifoldness, there are at least two components: *grāhya* and *grāhaka*. The sense of difference is produced by partial incompatibility between the two. The greater the variety of *grāhaka*-s, the greater the manifoldness of experiences.[102] The deepest reason for these incompatibilities is *vimarśa*. To put it in plain language, there is an inherent tendency to perceive the same object as a little bit different from itself each time it becomes an object of perception.

A reasonable objection to the postulate "the manifoldness is a result of divergences between *grāhaka* and correponding to it (or conformable to it) *grāhya*" is that some of the differentiation between stimuli is already hard-wired into organs of perception. We can tell a sound from a flash of light without any learning or projecting of some inner patterns. This objection is addressed by the following observation. There was an experiment made in which subjects were wearing up-down inverting spectacles. Initially, they were seeing everything upside-down. But with the passing of time an inversion occured, the normal perception returned despite wearing the glasses. When the subjects stopped wearing the glassses, they experienced another inversion and, thus, a restoration of normal vision. Thus, some mental structures, not the organs of perception, adapt the differentiation of "up-down" to become consistent with other activities. So, the view of *Pratyabhijñāhṛdayam* system is that all sources of stimulation are like space directions in a vacuum — there is a multitutde of them, but they are all the same.

[102]This might be observed when one takes lessons in drawing and starts noticing a lot of new details, imperfections, etc., in familiar pictures.

The differentiation is introduced during the interpretation called "perception." Some of the differentiating patterns might be given prenatally, for it is establsihed that newborns are capable of perception and making distinctions. But what is important, is that none of these patterns are hard-wired; they are merely a pre-existing biases.

When perceptual sense of difference is augmented with emotional biases, a sense of deeply personal differences of type "I"–"That" is born. The practical interest of this system is not in whether the white color might be learned to be perceived as red, but in whether the emotional and psycho-somatic influences on perception and cognition might be eliminated. The answer, in principle, is yes.

So, it is the patterns, priming the perception of the stream of sensations, that augment and filter *grāhya*, and create apparent discontinuities that define identities and differences between "things."

To reformulate this in technical terms, a *grāhaka*, being influenced by *pramātṛ*-s, results in *saṃjñā* by filtering of some aspects of *grāhya*, that are not compatible with those *pramātṛ*-s, and augmenting *grāhya* with features, compatible with active *pramātṛ*-s.

According to the predominance of various *tattva*-s, *pramātṛ*-s are traditionally classified into seven groups:

śiva

mantramaheśvara

mantreśvara

mantra

vijñānakala

pralayākala

sakala.

For details on the last four, see IPK 3.2.7-3.2.20. The practical importance of this classification is in the relative long-term stability of *pramātṛ*-s. This stability allows the detection and analysis of *pramātṛ*-s currently present.

चितिसंकोचात्मा चेतनोऽपि संकुचितविश्वमयः ॥ ४ ॥

citisaṃkocātmā cetano'pi saṃkucitaviśvamayaḥ || *4* ||

An autonomous instance of the contraction of *citi*, though capable of attentive awareness, contains within itself the Universe in an abbreviated (or contracted) form.

This *sūtra* addresses the questions of how *citi* might acquire a configuration that makes it limited, and how stable mental configurations are created. A reflection in a mirror, with which *citi* was compared in *sūtra* 2, cannot form stable entities nor can it become limited, without some other substance.

An autonomous instance of the contraction of *citi* is a process that restricts in real time the facilitation provided by *citi* to a portion of the perceptual space, and/or to a portion of the space of actions, and/or to a portion of the space of desires/emotions. This autonomous instance is, in essence, nothing but a part of *citi* that acts as an inhibitor[103] towards the whole of *citi*.

The first condition of self-limitation is given as "contraction," or abbreviation. This means that the energy of *śakti* should become relatively low in order to become trapped in a stable configuration.

The second condition is an isolation from other regions that makes a low energy configuration autonomous.

Once an autonomous instance of contraction of *citi* appears, the process of restriction of the facilitation (that is *citi*) becomes, with time, more automatic and robust.[104] By becoming well separated from other regions, it can withstand higher and higher levels of *śakti*, without starting to dissolve. Some of the autonomous instances are pre-existing at birth.

The autonomy and, thus, the multitude of active centers, are only apparent, since the source of the autonomy is in the nature of

[103] How can *citi* inhibit herself? It happens similarly to the way gravity acts against itself with the help of a weight scale, where a larger weight counteracts the gravitational force acting upon a smaller weight, so as to move it upwards. Another analogy is a sound wave reflected by another sound wave that has a very high intensity.

[104] Complex and multi-step psychological processes tend with time to assume a contracted and one-step form. For example, typing "the" is initially a sequence of separate actions: pressing letter "t," changing finger position for the letter "h," pressing "h" changing finger position for the letter "e," pressing "e." With practice, this process becomes contracted and forms a single gesture — typing the word "the."

citi, and *citi* is the one and the only active agent behind all mental activity. She *is* self-impelling.

Despite being limited, any such autonomous intance is capable of reflecting the whole. Thus, a limited individual, that results from multiple contractions, is still capable of the right conception that leads to the removal of all limitations.

Given the two conditions for the formation of autonomous instances, it is possible to devise a *yoga*, based on raising the level of *śakti* and on establishing deep analogies and correspondences between relatively isolated areas of experience. Such *yoga*-s exist in tantric traditions, where macrocosm–microcosm correspondences, images, integrating multiple modalities, and the use of all functions of the body to raise the level of *śakti* are all well articulated. Practices of *Pratyabhijñāhṛdayam* system use precise concentration of *śakti* on the barriers to dissolution. The instrument for such concentration is knowledge, gained on the path of *true reasoning.*

Each autonomous instance of contraction of *citi* undergoes cyclic transformations. Each cycle is a cycle of emission–persistence–contraction[105] that is only a restricted version of the same cycle with which *citi* manifests itself in creating the Universe.

In the sphere of emotions, an autonomous instance of contraction of *citi* emanates from the restricted at some point faculty to make everything a subject of cognition/contemplation/decision. In particular, when the ability to doubt everything is restricted, it causes the emergence of a particular autonomous instance of contraction of *citi* — Ego. The more restrictive the instance, the more it becomes Ego and is perceived as "I." As a consequence, the stronger the Ego, the more it resists a removal of the restrictions that give it its existence for the Ego is a self-imposed limitation that forbids questioning its own foundations.

The instances of contraction of *citi* exist in a variety of scales, from a single recollection (that is less vivid and detailed than the original impression) to major modes of consciousness, like sleep, meditative trance, hypnotic trance, etc.

Next, some major modes of consciousness will be discussed.

Ordinary consciousness has a variety of distinct instances the same way an actor plays a variety of roles. Just compare your "self" when you are in the company of your parents to your "self" when in the company of peers; or when you are on a deserted ocean beach as compared to in a business meeting. Your state of perceptive

[105] It might be compared to waves on ocean beach.

awareness is quite different in these cases.

Of the various states and modes that consciousness functions in, the phases of wakefulness, dreaming, deep sleep, and *the fourth* (*turīya*) deserve special attention. The short exposition below follows Swami Rama's book [Ram82], which is a commentary to *Māṇḍukya* upanishad.

The first mode of consciousness is the waking state, *vaiśvānara*. It tunes into the gross, external [stimuli].[106] The content of consciousness is filtered by the Ego and is characterized by subject–object polarization.

The second mode of consciousness is the dreaming state, *taijasa*. It tunes into the internal plane (fantasies, dreams, projections of desires) and partakes of isolation (from the gross and the external).[107] The subject–object duality is still present, but it is somewhat less rigid than in the waking state.

The third mode of consciousness is the abiding in deep sleep. When one is insensible [to external stimuli], desiring nothing and dreaming nothing, that state is the deep sleep.[108]

This third mode, called *prājña*, has no subject–object duality. It is an ocean of pure cognitions, saturated with bliss and experiencing it. It has only one aspect — attentiveness.[109] In this mode, the unconscious is in the scope of awareness, and the fog of perceptual experiences and memories is not present to interfere with knowing it.

These three modes might be called perceptual, imaginative, and conceptual states, correspondingly.

Breaking barriers between these states is important for reversing these contractions of *citi* and, thus, for dissolving their isolation and autonomy. In order to break these barriers one should transcend into another mode, or state of consciousness, called *the fourth* (*turīya*), which is the state *citi* contracted from into the three states.

The fourth is characterized as follows:
It is preeminent among all other states;
it experiences and knows every other state;

---

[106] *jāgaritasthāno bahiḥprajñaḥ saptāṅga ekonaviṃśatimukhaḥ sthūlabhugvaiśvānaraḥ prathamaḥ pādaḥ* ManUp.3

[107] *svapnasthāno'ntaprajñaḥ saptāṅga ekaviṃśatimukhaḥ praviviktabhuktaijaso dvitīyaḥ pādaḥ* ManUp.4

[108] *yatra supto na kañcana kāmaṃ kāmayate na kañcana svapnaṃ paśyati tatsuṣuptam* ManUp.5.a

[109] *suṣuptasthāna ekībhūtaḥ prajñānaghana evānandamayo hyānandabhuk cetomukhaḥ prājñastṛtīyaḥ pādaḥ* ManUp.5.b

it regulates the inner feelings;
it is the source of every other state;
in it is the origination and dissolution of all mental phenomena.[110]

One thinks of it as
neither tuning into the internal plane,
nor tuning into the external plane,
nor tuning into both planes at once;
as neither pure awareness,
nor attention,
nor non-attention;
as unobserved, not experienced during the ordinary course of life (unlike the three other states),
ungraspable by intuition,
having no prior signs (or symptoms).[111]

It is unimaginable, undefinable by means of verbal expression;
it consists primarily of self-supporting *buddhi*;
it is soothing the proliferation of illusions caused by the employment of language;
it is free from passions, happy, having no dualities. It is the real Self that is to be discerned in its pure form.[112]

Here is a practice that aims at breaking barriers between perceptual, imaginative, and conceptual states.

It is outlined in the *sūtra*-s 8-12 of the *Māṇḍūkya* upanishad. One has to realize that the waking state, *vaiśvānara*, is emphasized by concentration on *ājña-cakra* and by articulation of the sound *a*; that the dreaming state, *taijasa*, is emphasized by concentration on *viśuddha-cakra* and by articulation of the sound *u*; that the deep sleep state, *prājña*, is emphasized by concentration on *anāhata-cakra* and by articulation of the sound *ṃ*. Then, by articulation of *a-u-ṃ* with the corresponding shift of concentrated attention to *ājña-cakra* – *viśuddha-cakra* – *anāhata-cakra* for extended periods of time, the articulation of sounds is merged into *Oṁ*, and the consciousness is pulled towards *the fourth*. The shift to *prājña* should be learned. A practice to do this is called *yoga-nidrā*, or yogic sleep. Details might be found in [Ram96].

[110] *eṣa sarveśvara eṣasarvajña eṣo'ntaryāmyeṣa yoniḥ sarvasya prabhavāpyayau hi bhūtānām* ManUp.6

[111] *nāntaḥprajñaṃ na bahiṣprajñaṃ nobhayataḥprajñaṃ na prajñānaghanaṃ na prajñaṃ nāprajñamadṛṣṭamavyavahāryamagrāhyamalakśaṇaṃ* ManUp.7.a

[112] *acintyamavyapadeśyamekātmapratyayasāraṃ prapañcopaśamaṃ śāntaṃ śivamadvaitaṃ caturthaṃ manyante sa ātmā sa vijñeyaḥ* ManUp.7.b

चितिरेव चेतनपदादवरूढा चेत्यसंकोचिनी चित्तम् ॥ ५॥

citireva cetanapadādavarūḍhā cetyasaṃkocinī cittam || 5||

That same *citi*, descended from the loci of attention [and] shaped by the schematic (lit. "contracted") form of what has been perceived [becomes] *citta.*

A *citta* possesses the ability (*śakti*) to change itself, but there is not enough energy in it to become completely dissolved or to break limitations. It is like a puddle of water left after the tide has gone out — it acquires existence autonomous from the sea. What keeps it together are various *tattva*-s.

This *sūtra* describes the process of converting a short-term potentiation into a long-term one. First, there is a wave of energy, manifesting itself as a roaming perceptive attention. Next, through dissipation of the energy, the wave becomes trapped in a relatively stable and rigid configuration of percepts, actions, and feelings, linked together by mutual associations (which themselves are just a combination of *tattva*-s). Then, the components of this configuration become more abstract, or schematic, than the originals. As a result, the complex becomes active under more general circumstances than those at the initial wave of energy with which it arose.

It is *citi* (or long term facilitation of concentration of attention) that is the energy behind the *cittavṛtti*-s. Each autonomous instance of contraction of *citi* acts as a source of and defines a direction for each activation or mutation ("flow of associations"). Unrestrained by external stimuli and being influenced by many such autonomous instances, these cascading activations and mutations present themselves as dreams in sleep or as a pervasive but subtle net of delusions (*māyā*) when awake.

Re-identification of major instances of contraction of *citi* with *cit* (also called recognition of self-sameness of the Self), and restoration of middle-scale plasticity results in *citta-vṛtti-nirodha* (see YS.1.2)

तन्मयो मायाप्रमाता ॥ ६ ॥

tanmayo māyāpramātā || *6* ||

A *pramātṛ*, causing *māyā*, emanates from *citta*.

How is *māyā* created?

First of all, it needs a mechanism for inhibition. Inhibition can be of two kinds: direct inhibition and distraction. If inhibition is to be active in all experiences, even in the new and novel, both mechanisms are needed, for memories might be inhibited directly, but new pathways of recollection or new impressions require temporary distraction to allow direct inhibition to set in.

Secondly, there should be a motive or an impulse for an inhibition.

There are at least three sources of such motives or impulses. One is proximity or association with some mental "things," the inhibition of which was decided upon during, or triggered by some event in the past.

The other one is the conscious decision to forget or avoid some memories or ideas that are too painful, or are deemed plainly negative or unworthy.

The third one is a built-in mechanism that is triggered by conditions that might lead to or are already causing, a psychological trauma. When muscles are stretched beyond what they are habituated to, the neuromusclar apparatus sends them a signal to relax; it does this autonomously, without a conscious command. The same way, when a stimulus is too strong, or internal dissonance too violent, or when flows of *prāṇa*, *apāna*, etc. cause changes in mental processes that are too rapid or too unbalanced , an autonomuous inhibition, designed to protect *antakaraṇa*, is activated. In the case of a too strong stimulus, the reaction might be numbness or loss of sensitivity in some perceptual modality. In the case of a violent cognitive dissonance, it might be suppression of parts of the situation that cause the conflict. In the case of a violent emotional dissonance, the reaction might range from depression, to tears, to rage, to physiological stress, to fainting. In the case of too strong or disruptive flows[113] of *prāṇa*, *apāna*, etc., the defensive mecha-

[113]For example, unimpeded flows through *svādhiṣṭhāna-cakra* might bring under certain circumstances an image of "social, and thus verbose, self" in the likeness of the goddess Kali.

nism consists of activating volitional impulses that block the flows. These defensive mechanisms should not be disabled or interfered with, unless one has conscious command and control of specific methods of dealing with potentially traumatic experiences.

For additional notes on impulses for inhibition and how to deal with them, see Appendix B.

In order to understand sources of the motives or impulses to inhibit, one needs to contemplate what is a psychological crisis and what are the ways to resolve it. Here is a short schema.

A psychological crisis is created when a situation (S) imposes too strong of a limitation (L), as measured by the degree of "I-am-to-be-such" intent (D) and the time (T), meted out for realizing D.

T might be defined not only by objective characteristics of S, but by a *mātṛ* and *kañcuka*-s as well.

There are at least four ways to deal with such a crisis:

1. *a flight* to perform actions leading to the avoidance of S all together

2. *a fight* to perform actions that increase opportunities, ways and means to realize D in S

3. *a reduction of D* so that the same L does not cause a crisis

4. *an increase in T* if S allows it

The first way results in a major motive for long-term inhibition. It might be triggered on the instinctive level, especially by certain smells, or it might be decided upon as, subjectively, the best course of action. A consistent way to counteract existing long-term inhibitions, resulting from the flight reaction, is given by a verse[114] of Yoga Sutra:

> [*Samādhi* results] from the predisposition to direct mind
> inwards upon that which is on the verge of dominating,
> or overwhelming.[115]

The second way is feasible only if there is enough skill, means, and knowledge to make a fight, and if there is support from hypothalamic-pituitary-adrenal axis. One of the after-effects of

[114] *īśvarapraṇidhānādvā* YS.1.23

[115] This interpretation of YS.1.23 appears quite different from traditional interpretations. There is no real contradiction here, just a difference of projections onto different planes of practical meaning.

the fighting response (its *karma*) is an increase of personal values, associated with D, making ego stronger[116] and, thus, increasing the potential for a future crisis. Another after-effect is the inhibition of those constructs that were an expression of weakness during the fight. If the two after-effects of fighting are addressed afterwards, then fighting becomes a skillful way to deal with a crisis.

The third way requires skills of emotional self-regulation. The fourth way is done by psycho-physiological means[117] or by directly adjusting current expectations — whatever gives more space to untie the knot of the crisis.

The third and the fourth ways aim at a reconfiguration of the crisis situation, instead of inhibition or repression, which always result in a long-term loss of awareness. The knowledge and skills required for the third and the fourth ways of dealing with a crisis, are a part of the *Pratyabhijñā* system, but it is not the only system to do this — most Indian philosophies of liberation teach skills needed for the third and the fourth ways.

On a practical level, whenever one detects an inhibition of some ideas, memories, actions, etc., one should analyze what type of inhibition it is, what were the motives or impulses for it, and what are the sources of these motives or impulses. Once the sources are known, they might be weakened, reconfigured, or dissolved. The motives and inhibitions devoid of the sources are relatively easy to remove.

The existence of autonomic mechanisms for inhibition, that kick in when psychological tension becomes too high, means that one should move forward with *sādhana* one step at a time, avoiding shock experiences and too much continuous stress. For the same reason one should avoid changing lifestyle too abruptly.

Let's return to the origin of *māyā*.

An original source of inhibition is an experience that causes a psychological crisis. Any such crisis is characterized by a moment of high level energy, or *śakti*. When the level falls, the schematic representation of the crisis (S–L–D–T), augmented with structures that resolve it, forms a *citta* (see *sūtra* 5). If resolution was accomplished by means of inhibition, whether direct or through distrac-

[116] Osho once noticed (in *The Book of Secrets*), "It is difficult to find a yogi who is not an egoist. And yogis may go on talking about egolessness, but they cannot be egoless. The very process they go through creates the ego. The fight is the process."

[117] *Prāṇāyāma*, tantric visualizations, *mantra*-s, changes in the level of hormones like adrenalin, etc.

tion, whether intentional or autonomic, then this *citta* functions to avoid a re-occurrence of the crisis and to deflect most of the energy, if it does occur. With time, it becomes augmented with more and more detecting structures that evaluate a potential for a crisis, and with more and more deflecting structures (also called defense mechanisms). Because of this generalization, the complex becomes a *pramātṛ*, which is a stable and robust source of *māyā*.

There are three major mechanisms[118] to counteract the effects of *citta* and, in particular, to remove a support from a *pramātṛ*. The first is called *āṇavaḥ visargaḥ*, or repose, or abatement of *citta* (attainable by deep relaxation and/or distraction). The second is called *śāktaḥ visargaḥ*, or full understanding of *citta* structure. The third is called *śāṃbhavaḥ visargaḥ*, or dissolution of *citta*. Each mechanism gives a name for a group of techniques, based primarily on that mechanism.

An important specific mechanism that gives rise to the *māyā* involves illusions staged by the Ego.

A focused expression of free will along a very limited and directional kernel (as expressed, for example, by the sentiment "this is exactly what I want," followed by the resolve to obtain it) has an effect of detachment from many other points of expression, it was attached to. This detachment results in a temporary increase in the mobility of free will, which in turn results in an expression of *ānandaśakti* and, thus, in an experience of *camatkāra*. Therefore, if one is ignorant of this mechanism, or not observant of it, the Ego presents itself as the gate to the garden of bliss. But the Ego is capable of opening it only in the presence of a strong opposition, so that a strong movement of attaching to one ideal causes pronounced detachment from others. The new attachment, if actively pursued after the dissipation of *camatkāra*, becomes a driver of behaviour. It becomes binding and therefore causes unease, turning into suffering. In order to open that gate another strong opposition to repeat pronounced detachment, is required. The Ego, therefore, is always on a quest to find strong dualities. Mistaking this recurring illusion, staged by the Ego, for the ultimate and natural state of Self is the primordial ignorance (*avijjā* (P)), which is the root of all suffering (see commentary to *sūtra* 8).

[118] *sa ca eṣa visargastridhā*
āṇavaḥ cittaviśrāntirūpaḥ
śāktaḥ cittasaṃbodhalakṣaṇaḥ
śāṃbhavaḥ cittapralayarūpaḥ AbhTs 3.25

स चैको द्विरूपस्त्रिमयश्चतुरात्मा सप्तपञ्चकस्वभावः ॥ ७॥

sa caiko dvirūpastrimayaścaturātmā saptapañcakasvabhāvaḥ || 7||

That *pramātṛ*, [though it is] self-same [for, in substance, it is nothing but *cit*], has two forms [as an illumination and as a veil], and three expressions (as *āṇavamala, māyīyamala kārmamala*). It has four functional frames (in the space of *saṃskāra*-s, in the subtle energies *prāṇa, apāna*, etc., in *puryaṣṭaka*, and in *śarīra*), and its inherent disposition is [the unfoldment] of the 35 *tattva*-s.

This gives a paradigm for investigation. The goal of the investigation is to determine the structure and dynamic of those mental phenomena that are the cause of suffering.

What I habitually refer to as "I" or "my self" is a *pramātṛ*. The filtering and augmentation, performed by this *pramātṛ*, is perceived as self-expression.

1. As there are usually more than one *pramātṛ*, concurrence between them causes internal conflicts that result in attitudes like "this is mine – that is not," even when related to one's own feelings, ideas, or actions. The first step of any analysis is to accept as an axiom that all feelings, ideas and actions, no matter how aversive or strange, are but the consequences and expressions of one's own free will.

2. The second step is to identify attention biases (what is noticed, what is not ignored), and how "self" is being expressed through this selectivity. What do you accept without questioning and what thoughts you do not dare to think?

3. The third step is to analyze the persistent attention biases as expressions of various *mala*-s.

4. Next, one should analyze expressions of *mala*-s, and the composition of *mala*-s, from the point of view of the four functional frames of references. For exapmle, what[119] is behind the recurrence of a particular *mala* that was once deconstructed? How does arising of certain ideas cause a shortness of breath or yawning or stomach troubles? What causes elevated sensitivity, or lack of it, to particular colors, smells, sounds, etc.? How transient pains in the spine relate to the stress of social interactions?

[119]Which *saṃskāra*?

5. Finally, all constructs and manifestations are to be resolved into configurations of the 35 *tattva*-s, following the *śivatattva*. Practically important is discernment of only those *tattva*-s that make the constructs specific and rigid; in particular, it is important to analyze *kañcuka*-s protecting the *pramātṛ*.

तद्भूमिकाः सर्वदर्शनस्थितयः ॥ ८ ॥

tadbhūmikāḥ sarvadarśanasthitayaḥ || *8* ||

Established prepositions of all systems of philosophy (and of all personally held views) are expressing various combinations of the 35 *tattva*-s (all, following *śivatattva*).

For example, a materialistic view that postulates that mental faculties are a reflection of the material Universe in itself, is expressive of *karmendriya*-s, *jñānendriya*-s, *tanmātra*-s, and *mahābhūta*-s.

The philosophical system of *Sāṃkhya* is expressive of *puruṣatattva* and all *tattva*-s below it.

The schema of dependent co-arising (see *paṭiccasamuppādasutta* SN XII.1), which is central to the Bauddha dharma, might be represented in the following fashion. Here (P) denotes Pali words; $\propto$ means "is a requisite condition of".

1. *avijjā* **(P)** $\propto$ *saṅkhārā* **(P)** *avijjā* (P), or experiential ignorance of the causes and pathways of suffering (*duḥkha*), is an expression of *māyātattva*. *saṅkhārā* (P) is a heap of *saṃskāra*-s.

   Thus, 1. means that *māyātattva* is a prerequisite condition for composites, consisting of the the five *kañcuka*-s.

2. *saṅkhārā* **(P)** $\propto$ *viññāṇa* **(P)** *viññāṇa* (P), or perceptual predisposition, an idea embossed in consciousness, a groove in present and future distribution of attention, is a *pramātṛ* of either *sakala* or *pralayākala* types with a pronounced presence of *vidyātattva*.

   viññāṇa (P) (Sanskrit equivalent is *vijñāna*) fragments the contiguous stream of stimulation into bits and pieces, and isolates some of them for out-of-context perception. For the purpose of analysis, the most important quality of *viññāṇa* (P) is that it separates and highlights a fragment of a perceptual image in a way that enables the fragment to be perceived, associated, and connected with other mental constructs in the absence of the original image.[120]

   Thus, 2. means that *saṃskāra*-s are a requisite condition for *sakala-pramātṛ*-s and for *pralayākala-pramātṛ*-s.

[120] For example, realizing that the apple, just tasted, is sweet tasting, is an instance of *vijñāna*.

3. *viññāṇa* **(P)** $\propto$ *nāmarūpa* **(P)** *nāmarūpa* (P), or individual being as a composite of immaterial and material factors, is a manifest duality of *puruṣatattva* vs. *prakṛtitattva*.

Thus, 3. means that a *pramātṛ* of either *sakala* or *pralayākala* type is a requisite condition for the manifest duality *puruṣa* vs. *prakṛti*.

4. *nāmarūpa* **(P)** $\propto$ *salāyatana* **(P)** *salāyatana* (P), or the six sense bases, are the five *tanmātra*-s with corresponding *jñānendriya*-s and the *manastattva*.

Thus, 4. means that the manifest duality *puruṣa* vs. *prakṛti* is a requisite condition for the divergence of experience into the six modalities.

5. *salāyatana* **(P)** $\propto$ *phassa* **(P)** *phassa* (P) is a contact, or sense-impression (defined as coming together of *viññāṇa* (P), *salāyatana* (P) and a stream of stimulation). A stream of stimulation is expressed as composite of *mahābhūta* with *jñānendriya*-s. *phassa* (P) is part of the act of *sthiti* (see sutra 10).

Thus, 5. means that by definition, *salāyatana* (P) is a requisite condition of *phassa* (P).

6. *phassa* **(P)** $\propto$ *vedanā* **(P)** *vedanā* (P) is a feeling. *vedanā* (P) is a complex of one or more *phassa*-s augmented with *śuddhavidyātattva*. *vedanā* (P) has three distinct vertexes: pleasure, pain, and indifference. In any case it is a relation of perceptual experience to a like–dislike axis.

Thus, 6. means that a sense-impression is a requisite condition of a feeling.

7. *vedanā* **(P)** $\propto$ *taṇhā* **(P)** *taṇhā* (P), or the fever of unsatisfied longing. *taṇhā* (P) is a *vedanā* (P) augmented with *rāgatattva* and *niyatitattva*. Te distinct characteristic of *taṇhā* (P) is the potential to make behaviour driven by a single idea or craving, making it almost one-dimensional.

Thus, 7. means that a feeling, is a requisite condition for the fever of unsatisfied longing.

8. *taṇhā* **(P)** $\propto$ *upādāna* **(P)** *upādāna* (P), or grasping, by means of which a desire is kept alive; an addiction. The "grasping" here means a *relish* of a preference to enjoy or to avoid. *upādāna* (P) is a *citta* grown around a *taṇhā* (P).

Thus, 8. means that the fever of unsatisfied longing is a requisite condition for an addiction, for grasping, by means of which a desire is kept alive.

taṇhā (P) is requisite for the formation of an *upādāna* (P). A ghost of experienced *taṇhā* (P) is what animates an *upādāna* (P). Once grown, *upādāna* (P) might perpetuate itself, even if the *taṇhā* (P) is no longer there. This continuous existence of *upādāna* is caused by mutual activation of *citta* components.

9. ***upādāna* (P) $\propto$ *bhava* (P)** *bhava* (P), or becoming, is a stable and focused deflection of *icchāśakti* onto *antaḥkaraṇa* by *īśvaratattva*. The deflection is made stable and focused by an *upādāna* (P).

Thus, 9. means that the grasping, by means of which a desire is kept alive, is a requisite condition for making a "That"-disposition of thought stable and focused.

10. ***bhava* (P) $\propto$ *jāti* (P)** *jāti* (P), or birth, rebirth, entering a *saṃsāra*. The limitation, characteristic of *jāti*, is dominated by *ahaṃkāratattva*. To understand the concept of *jāti* (P), one needs to consider it on a variety of time scales (see *saṃsāra*) and think beyond a physical body.

Thus, 10. means that a stable and focused deflection of *icchāśakti* onto *antaḥkaraṇa* is a requisite condition for entering a *saṃsāra*.

Yet another requisite condition for entering a *saṃsāra* is a *tirodhāna* in the form of a notion of *self*, pervading the spheres of desires, actions and experiences. Deconstruction of all such notions of *self* is called in Buddhism attaining "*anatta* (P)."

11. ***jāti* (P) $\propto$ *jarā* (P), *maraṇa* (P), *soka* (P), ...** the whole heap of suffering. Thus, 11. means that entering a *saṃsāra* is a requisite condition for the whole heap of suffering.

Here, as in Buddhism, suffering is distinguished from pain: Buddha experienced pain but he did not suffer. Suffering originates with mind. Physical pain is just a pretext for suffering. "The whole heap of suffering" is but a consequence of the *āṇavamala*.

When using the eleven links of the schema of dependent co-arising for practical analysis of experiences, the correct order is the order of discovery (*pratiloma*), which is the reverse of the sequence 1–11. One starts with a concrete case of suffering, anguish or despair. Then one has to find what particular instance of *saṃsāra* the suffering manifests in, and recollect the moment of entering it. Then, one has to reflect upon the dynamic (*bhava* (P)) of entering a stream of *saṃsāra*. From that, one infers existence of an *upādāna* (P), and from understanding the details of it, one looks for a *taṇhā* (P) that was the seed of the *upādāna* (P). After identifying the *taṇhā* (P), one has to recollect *vedanā*-s (P) that coalesced in this *taṇhā* (P). After recalling these *vedanā*-s (P) to the point of reliving them, one has to recall particular sense impressions that gave rise to the *vedanā*-s (P). Then, one has to analyze what features[121] of those sense impressions were giving rise to the feelings, determining if it was a partucular smell, body curve, tone of the voice, texture, taste, or relevance to a cherished idea, and noticing, in particular, whether it was related to physiological needs or to the sphere of ideas. Then, one has to find out[122] what was behind those feelings — physiological needs, memories, habits, biases, some conceptual ideas about good or bad, etc. Next, one has to contemplate[123] how those ideas or features become formed to be separate from the original, only slightly differentiated, flow of stimulation. Next, one has to find out[124] what *saṃskāra*-s are the driving force behind the process of abstraction that is the *viññāṇa* (P). And, finally, one has to uncover[125] the mechanisms that conceal the composition and the influence of *saṃskāra*-s. After all the links are uncovered, one has to replay it in his mind from step 1 to 11 in order to understand how the suffering came to be. This understanding will result in detachment and dispassion (*vairagya*).

The above shows that the conceptual system of the *Pratyabhijñā* is capable of expressing the schema of dependent co-arising, and that there are no direct contradictions between the two. Which schema should be used — the schema of dependent co-arising or the unfolding of the five acts by means of the 35 *tattva*-s? Whatever aids in the analysis of a particular behavioral pattern and leads to the unwinding or deconstruction of mental formations that are causing ignorance and suffering. I've found it beneficial to apply both schemas to some hard problems, since they highlight different

[121]This is the analysis of *salāyatana* (P) $\propto$ *phassa* (P) link.

[122]This is the analysis of *nāmarūpa* (P) $\propto$ *salāyatana* (P) link.

[123]This is the analysis of *viññāṇa* (P) $\propto$ *nāmarūpa* (P) link.

[124]This is the analysis of *saṅkhārā* (P) $\propto$ *viññāṇa* (P) link. The practice of *yoga-nidrā* is a good way to make *saṃskāra*-s apparent.

[125]This is the analysis of *avijjā* (P) $\propto$ *saṅkhārā* (P). See entry for *kañcuka* for some of the mechanisms.

aspects. The schema of dependent co-arising makes it easier to detect patterns of manifestation, while the conceptual system of the *Pratyabhijñā* provides an analysis that enables transformations of the patterns.

Some natural questions arise at this point: why are there multiple systems of philosophy, all having the same goal? Why are there multiple paradigms and principles? Are different formulations equivalent, or at least compatible?

The purpose of a conceptual system is to provide a consistent and effective *instrumentation* for formation, detection, and controlled activation of mental formations, leading to the goal (enligtenment).

To be useful for treading a path, a conceptual system should bring under investigation and make subject to transformation those mental formations that were not analyzable or transformable in one's practice without it. Which instrumentation is effective and feasible, depends greatly on one's *karma*, *prakṛti*, education, profession, teachers, community of peers, etc. A variety of these conditions is the cause of the variety of paradigms and philosophical systems of liberation.

Any system of philosophy should be represented as a set of paradigms, schemas, principles and practices comprising it, even if such representation is incomplete. Then, paradigms, schemas, and principles should be reconstructed on the internal plane as knowledge (see *buddhi*) in order to become an instrumentation. It is the effectiveness of *instrumentation* — not the expressiveness (that is, not the ability to formulate any phenomena in terms of the system), not an analytic precision, not being part of a respected tradition — that has a direct pragmatic value for a *sādhana*.

Scripts and practices are not overly dependent on a philosophical system and many are shared between various traditions. The fruits of practices and the interpretation of failures to acquire the fruits are, however, quite dependent on the philosophical system one uses as a guide. As long as there are no major contradictions with one's primary philosophical system, anything that works for a particular problem, might be used. Above all, Indian doctrines of liberation are geared towards procedural effeciveness.

Errors and failures due to inadequate understanding of concepts or due to erroneous concepts are the most difficult to detect and correct. Therefore, it is important to check what effect practices have on internalized basic concepts and to revise practices if concepts are being distorted.

चिद्वत्तच्छक्तिसंकोचात् मलावृतः संसारी ॥ ९ ॥

cidvattacchaktisaṃkocāt malāvṛtaḥ saṃsārī || 9||

[Though] being nothing but *cit*, [*pramātṛ*] enveloped with *mala*-s, because of a contraction of *śakti*, [becomes] a *saṃsārin*.

An important requisite condition for *jāti* (P), or entering a *saṃsāra*, is "being enveloped with *mala*-s." Transcending *saṃsāra*, then, requires a purging of *mala*-s. There are three types of *mala*-s, but multiple specific instances. To dissolve them is quite a lengthy process. As Dhammapada[126] puts it,

> One by one, little by little, moment by moment,
> a wise man should remove his own impurities,
> as a smith removes dross from silver.

Not any manifestation results in *saṃsāra*, only that where contraction of *śakti* results in *mala*-s. So, he who is liberated is still capable of living and experiencing — by being free of *mala*-s, he will remain free from *saṃsāra*.

---

[126]DhP XVIII.239

तथापि तद्वत्पञ्चकृत्यानि करोति ॥ १० ॥

tathāpi tadvatpañcakṛtyāni karoti || 10||

Notwithstanding [becoming a *saṃsārin*], he (*pramātṛ*), being homologous to *cit*, effects the five actions.

As noted in Tantraloka,[127] the five actions are:

sṛṣṭi	emission;
sthiti	maintaining the expansion;
tirodhāna	setting aside by means of an opposition, or duality;
saṃhāra	retraction, or contracting of *śakti*;
anugraha	unwinding into an effortless and direct awareness of the intrinsic unity of *cit*. *Anugraha* is usually translated as "grace," which reflects the non-intentional nature of this action.

sṛṣṭi, *sthiti*, and *saṃhāra* constitute the fundamental cycle of the processes of manifestation. *tirodhāna* results, after *saṃhāra*, in arising of *saṃskāra*-s, which are seeds of *karma*. Buddha said[128]:

> The passion for his resolves is a man's sensuality, not
> the beautiful sensual pleasures found in the world.

It is this passion for one's own resolves that is *tirodhāna*. A resolve creates an intellectual distinction, separation, or opposition, but the passion (*rāga*) in maintaining the resolve makes it personal, makes it part of the Ego, and thus very difficult to dissolve. *Tirodhāna* is a fault, created by an *āṇavamala*.

On a psycho-physiological level, *tirodhāna* is established when memories, emotions and reactions caused by an event settle down (typical time frame 20 min – 1 day).

Of all the five actions, *anugraha* is the rarest. *anugraha* "burns" *saṃskāra*-s, and, in this sense, is opposite to *tirodhāna*. Through *anugraha*, *saṃskāra*-s lose the source of support and, therefore, tend to fade away. The *Pratyabhijñā* system aims at creating conditions for *anugraha* to occur for every instance of *tirodhāna*. When

---

[127] *sṛṣṭisthititirodhānasaṃhārānugrahādica* TA.1.79.a

[128] AN III.99, translated by Thanissaro Bhikkhu

anugraha does occur for every instance of *tirodhāna* — that is enlightenment.

These five actions are present on various planes of manifestation and in different time frames. At the stage of *sthiti*, another process of manifestation could spring up. This imbedded branching creates a tree-like dynamic structure of interconnected processes, having various time frames.

Here is an example of a process, which includes all of these five actions, on the plane of personal preferences and on the scale of several minutes.

Let's imagine that you wandered by chance into a library room and realized that there might be interesting books in there. Memories, wishes, skills, tasks, curiosity, etc., related to reading are stirred up in you. This is a *sṛṣṭi*. You start browsing bookshelves, opening this book, that book, reading a paragraph, looking at illustrations, etc. This is a *sthiti*. Then you come across a book that is antique, beautiful and fascinates you so much that you spend a couple of hours reading it; and you form an opinion that this book is the most precious book in the library. That is a *tirodhāna*. Next, you are invited to have a cup of tea, and that distracts you from all thoughts about the book, however, when the conversation touches upon books, the memory of beautiful antique book instantly comes to mind. This is a *saṃhāra*. After you leave the house, a thought occurs to you that there were many other books in that library, that, judging by the tastes of its owner, should be at least as interesting as the one that fascinated you. The sense that that one book is somehow separate from all others disappears. Your curiosity shifts from that book back to the whole library, and no attachment remains to the book. That is an *anugraha*.

Since *anugraha* means also "grace," there is a danger of extroversion. As Swami Rama wrote in [Ram82],

> In religions, grace is considered to be a gift bestowed on the seeker, either as a reward for following the commandments or by mere whim. Thus, the bestowing of blessings serves as a bribe to make one conform, and it implies that the seeker is helpless to succeed by his own effort. ...Fear and insecurity are the logical results.

There is no effort involved in attaining *anugraha*, only relaxation of one's efforts.

आभासनरक्तिविमर्शनबीजावस्थापनविलापनतस्तानि ॥ ११ ॥

ābhāsanaraktivimarśanabījāvasthāpanavilāpanatastāni || *11* ||

These [five actions] are accomplished

[in the case of *sṛṣṭi*] by making apparent a potential for an expansion;

[in the case of *sthiti*] by taking fancy in, relishing the opportunities;

[in the case of *saṃhāra*] by shifting, non-uniform self-reflection, that is alternating between affection and detachment;

[in the case of *tirodhāna*] by setting aside an object of the expansion by augmenting an opposition, or duality, onto the inner reflection of the object;

[in the case of *anugraha*] by dissolving [the duality through direct recognition of the intrinsic unity of *cit*].

If *saṃhāra* follows right after *tirodhāna*, then it creates *saṃskāra*-s, and they, in turn, become seeds of *saṃsāra*.

In order to dissolve these *saṃskāra*-s, one needs to reverse *saṃhāra* by precise *sṛṣṭi*, and to experience an *anugraha*, negating the *tirodhāna*.

तदपरिज्ञाने स्वशक्तिभिर्व्यामोहितता संसारित्वम् ॥ १२॥

tadaparijñāne svaśaktibhirvyāmohitatā saṃsāritvam || 12||

When lacking thorough practical knowledge of that,[129] being bewildered by one's own capabilities is being a *saṃsārin.*

As is said in HYP.3.107[130], "She (*śakti*) is for binding those who are of bewildered mind and for liberating of yogis."

When the lack of freedom is caused by external circumstances, it is easy to perceive. It is a bit more difficult to perceive when it is caused by the lack of one's own abilities. Doing something simply because you can do it, especially if you do it well, is not even thought of as a loss of freedom, but it might be, if one lacks practical knowledge of how the five acts are performed.

Freedom, among other things, is freedom to make a choice that is not the best, or not reasonable, or not practical. The mere realization "I *can* do that" or "this is *the best* possible course of action" or "this is *the truth*" binds one no less than helplessness and external constraints. This binding is caused by the act of *tirodhana.*

The moment one decides to do something, it seems the only correct thing to do. The moment one expresses a desire or an aversion, the relevance of one's own preferences becomes the unquestioned ultimate truth. "The moment we want to believe something, we suddenly see all the arguments for it, and become blind to the arguments against it."[131]

The realizations "I *can* do that," etc., are a good starting point of any analysis, since they are relatively easy recollected.

---

[129] how the five actions are accomplished

[130] *kandordhve kuṇḍalī śaktiḥ suptā mokṣāya yoginām |*
bandhanāya ca mūḍhanāṃ yastāṃ vetti sa yogavit ||

[131] George Bernard Shaw

तत्परिज्ञाने चित्तमेव अन्तर्मुखीभावेन चेतनपदाध्यारोहात् चितिः ॥ १३॥

tatparijñāne cittameva antarmukhībhāvena cetanapadādhyārohāt citiḥ || 13||

When having thorough practical knowledge of that[132], that same *citta*, by transition to introversion [regains the unimpeded configuration of] *citi.*

The transition starts with ascending to a state of being conscious of previously subconscious activations. Ascending to the state of being conscious can easily be observed during an interruption of an automatic action. Meditation is a way to interrupt many automatic processes so that they can be brought into the conscious plane.

This and the next two *sūtra*-s give the general principle for reconfiguration of mental processes and constructs. First, identify a process or a construct by means of analysis, using paradigms, principles, and schemas of the philosophical system. The identity is most often established as a mental pointer "this" rather than with words, since words distort what they refer to. Next, bring various components of the identified process into consciousness by means of an interruption or by means of the contrast between expected association, or relation, and the actual one. Then, maintain undivided attention on each component to make it slowly dissolve.

The *modus operandi* of *Pratyabhijñā* practices is "introvert and de-automatize."

[132]how the five actions are accomplished

चितिवह्निरवरोहपदे छन्नोऽपि मात्रया मेयेन्धनं प्लुष्यति ॥ १४॥

citivahnirarohapade channo'pi mātrayā meyendhanaṃ plusyati || *14* ||

The fire of *citi*, though obscured when opportunities for flames to climb up are lacking, still slightly burns the kindling of *meya*.

This metaphorical expression means the following: the disintegrative power of a sustained, deliberate attention, though concealed when there is no strong focus for it, still dissolves in some degree the framework of filters, contexts, and biases that is maintained by a *pramātṛ*.

Attention here is called "the fire of *citi*" and is likened to tongues of fire — the flames that rise up when something burns. Similarly, when there are some focal points for attention to anchor in, then attention spreads over stimuli.

The practical importance of this quality of attention is that sustained attention by itself has the power to reduce the strength of associations and reflex-like connections, that have the strength of an automatism. To de-automatize a link $X \rightarrow Y$ sustain attention on the link.

Various practices, central to which is a sustained deliberate attention, are called *dhāraṇa*-s. *Vijñānabhairava* contains many such practices.

बललाभे विश्वमात्मसात्करोति ॥ १५॥

balalābhe viśvamātmasātkaroti || 15||

When [the fire of *citi*] acquires strength, it takes possession of everything.

In particular, it removes oppositions, or dualities, like external–internal, mine–not mine, etc., that were created by *tirodhāna*-s.

चिदानन्दलाभे देहादिषु चेत्यमानेष्वपि
चिदैकात्म्यप्रतिपत्तिदार्ढ्यं जीवन्मुक्तिः ॥ १६ ॥

cidānandalābhe dehādiṣu cetyamāneṣvapi
cidaikātmyapratipattidārḍhyaṃ jīvanmuktiḥ || 16||

Upon obtaining the bliss of *cit*, the robustness and unwavering sharpness of understanding of the selfsameness of *cit* in all (external and internal) perceivable manifestations (like the body, *prāṇa*-s, cognitive processes, etc.) [ripens into] the liberation while living.

Therefore, a merely intellectual ascertainment of the selfsameness of *cit* is not enough for liberation. Attainment of the bliss inherent in *cit* is needed as well.

Bliss is not in attaining an object of desire, but, rather in the release of *citi* from any purpose, intent, desire, attachment, etc. Attainment of the object of desire, or realization of intent, or fulfilling a purpose — all are just triggers of the release.

There are types of liberation that are attained at death of the physical body. This one occurs while one is still alive.

मध्यविकासाच्चिदानन्दलाभः ॥ १७ ॥

madhyavikāsāccidānandalābhaḥ || *17*||

Acquisition of the bliss of *cit* [starts with] the opening of the middle channel.

"The middle channel" is another name for *suṣumnā*. "Opening" it means that *prāṇa* and *apāna* start flowing though it, rather than through *iḍā* and *piṅgalā*. To open it, obstructions of a psycho-physiological nature must be removed.

This sutra points out a very important part of the process of liberation: reconfiguring physiology in accordance with the desired psychological changes. In order to effect lasting changes on the psychological plane, one has to make lasting changes on the physiological plane.

विकल्पक्षयशक्तिसंकोचविकासवाहच्छेदाद्यन्तकोटिनिभालनादय इहोपायाः ॥ १८ ॥

vikalpakṣayaśaktisaṃkocavikāsavāhacchedādyantakoṭinibhālanādaya ihopāyāḥ || 18||

Diminution of *vikalpa*-s, contraction/expansion [of *śakti*], cutting off flows [of *vayu*-s], seeing with the mind's eye the beginning and ending points, etc., in this case are methods [of attaining the opening of the middle channel].

Diminution of *vikalpa*-s is the primary practice of this system. It is described in the entry *vikalpa*.

Contraction/expansion of *śakti* means here the simultaneous expansion and contraction that is performed by *bhairavī mudrā*, as described in the commentary to this *sūtra*: "Attention is concentrated on an internal object, but sense organs are fully open to external objects, while keeping open eyes from winking or wandering."[133]

One technique for "cutting off flows of *vayu-s*" is described in the commentary as follows: Both *vāyu*-s (meaning *prāṇa* and *apāna*) should be prevented from flowing through *iḍā* and *piṅgalā* by inwardly muttering soundless sounds *k* or *h*, devoid of any vowels.

Another technique is described in *Śāktavijñānam* of Somananda as follows: "If one were to throw *manas* into the *kanda* by constraining both *prāṇa* and *apāna*, and then, having obtained a single pathway for both *vāyu*-s, one were to direct those flows into the middle channel, that would trigger the opening of the middle channel, resulting in *samādhi*. *Kanda* is situated in the *svādhiṣṭhāna cakra*, five and a half thumb widths below the navel."[134]

"Seeing with the mind's eye the beginning and ending points" means mentally following the trajectory of breath in a very specific manner. The attention is fully concentrated on a moving spot, the size of a thumb width. The trajectory of that spot starts

---

[133] *antarlakṣyo bahirdṛṣṭiḥ nimeṣonmeṣavarjitaḥ*

[134] *nābhyadha aṅgulāḥ pañca | meḍhrasyordhvāṅguladvayam ||*
tanmadhye kandanāmā ca | cakrasthānamiti smṛtam ||
prāṇāpānanirodhena | manastatraiva niḥkṣipet ||
samyagvāyugatiṃ jitvā | yāvanmadhyagatāṃ nayet ||
eṣa praveśa ityāhu

with the beginning of inhalation and originates in a spot called *dvādaśānta.*[135] It ends in *anāhata-cakra*[136] at the end of inhalation. During exhalation the trajectory is the reverse, starting in *anāhata-cakra* and ending in *dvādaśānta.* Attention should be kept steady during the transition from inhalation to exhalation and the transition from exhalation to inhalation.

"Etc." refers to the many techniques given in the ancient *Vijñānabhairava* tantra.

[135]It is found twelve thumb widths from the tip of the nose, right outside of the sternum.

[136]It is inside the body, right between the nipples.

समाधिसंस्कारवति व्युत्थाने भूयोभूयश्चिदैक्या
मर्शान्नित्योदितसमाधिलाभः ॥ १९ ॥

samādhisaṃskāravati vyutthāne bhūyobhūyaścidaikyā
marśānnityoditasamādhilābhaḥ || *19*||

From repeated direct experience of the selfsameness of *cit* in the *vyutthāna* state that is like a catalyst for [entering] *samādhi*, [comes] attaining of the perpetually experienced *samādhi*.

"Directly experiencing" here means "perceiving the identity of *cit* in two instances that appear to be different, without the aid of intermediate constructs."[137]

Selfsameness of *cit* is experienced whenever continuity among seemingly different things is perceived. Awareness during *anugraha* and observation of its effects provide the experience of the selfsameness in the plane of acts of free will.

[137] Such as verbal concepts or formulas like "*cit* is the same in both instances." Verbal/symbolic aids might be used, however, to bring both instances into short-term memory.

तदा प्रकाशानन्दसारमहामन्त्रवीर्यात्मकपूर्णाहन्तावेशात्
सदा सर्वसर्गसंहारकारिनिजसंविद्देवताचक्रेश्वरताप्राप्तिर्भवतीति
शिवम् ॥ २० ॥

tadā prakāśānandasāramahāmantravīryātmakapūrṇāhantāveśāt
sadā sarvasargasaṃhārakārinijasaṃviddevatācakreśvaratāprāptir
bhavatīti śivam || 20 ||

Then (when continually experienced *samādhi* is acquired) the acquisition of control over the whole spectrum of *devatā*-s, emanating from that innate *saṃvid*, which is conjuring all cycles of expansion-contraction, is being invariably transformed into the bliss of final liberation. The transformation stems from becoming absorbed into the complete-in-itself state of being, the state which imparts efficacy to the great *mantra* and whose quintessence is the bliss of *prakāśa*.

"The great *mantra*" is the *mantra ahaṃ* The literal meaning of it is "I am".

अहं

Appendix A.

Social networks and hierarchies

To establish and to become included into social hierarchies, to be a part of social networks, are built-in behavioral programs,[138] that one has to become aware of and has to understand in order to substantially increase the awareness of many sources of suffering.

Here we are interested only in how social networks are reflected in one's being, not in group dynamics, politics, religion, or economy. And they are reflected, directly or indirectly, in every aspect of a human being: psychological, psycho-physiological and physiological. They affect reasoning, perception, emotions, passions, self-respect, sense of well-being, etc. They affect mood, breathing, relaxation, sleep, etc. They affect expression of hormones, activity of glands, pain in the spine, tooth decay, digestion, blood pressure, etc.

The following is a short schema that I have found useful for analyzing these reflections.

There are two basic concepts: the mirror and the territory.

A *mirror* is a representation of another person's emotions, ideas, expressions of will, etc. It might be thought of as an integral internalized representation that can be attributed with perception, desires and activity of its own.

Due to such mirrors, one is able to become conscious of the feelings, thoughts, and intentions of another without any guessing or interpretation, or to engage in an inner dialog with an absent person; or to imagine how another would feel if one undertook certain actions, etc.

In general, a mirror can be a mirror of a sentient being, not necessarily of a human.

Inhibition of particular mirrors might be a consequence of emotional conflicts, facilitated by those mirrors. Such inhibition should be detected and skillfully avoided by practices such as the Buddhist practice of metta (compassion) and *ahiṃsā* (the principle of non-violence to all sentient beings, including one's self).

Robust connections of mirror images with inner planes of knowledge, emotions, and volitions are protected by *kañcukas*-s. For example, reflections into the plane of knowledge are effectively created by verbal formulas and are protected by automatic triggering

[138] A "program" here is not something hardwired and not subject to change — it is merely a bias that might be unlearned.

of deductions; by the assumption of validity of particular opinions, given a positive prior experience; by abstraction from context of validity of knowledge, and by the assumption that a knowledge deemed valid necessitates action that accords with it.

A *territory* is a node in a social network. It might be a real territory; it might be a voice in making certain decisions, it might be an amount of admiration from others, etc. In general, it is some resource, acquisition, or preservation of which depends on actions or attitudes of other people or sentient beings. A resource might be material, like food, shelter, safety, sex, etc., or it might be virtual, like being an object of admiration or attention, being an authority, etc., or it might be a future potential for the material or virtual resources. The idea of a territory seems to be either built-in or learned at a very early age on a non-conceptual level.

The expansion of a territory, attributed to self, evokes positive emotions, like elation, buoyancy, being accepted, etc., while either absolute or relative contraction of one's own territory causes various negative emotions, like envy, fear, anxiety, dejection, etc. If a perceived territory is different from how it is reflected in other people's mirrors, it causes internal conflicts, anger, neurosis, etc.

Social hierarchy is a relatively stable way to manage changes to territories without direct confrontation between members of the hierarchy.

When territories are represented in the mind, they are of two distinct flavors: those projecting outside and those projecting inside. A representation of a territory, projecting inside, transfers the energy of intentions, actions and emotions (reflected in mirrors corresponding to some members of a social network) onto one's own perceptions, actions, and emotions.[139] The active agent in a territory projecting inside is referred to as "they," " he," "she."

A representation of a territory, projecting outside, is a construct that one's expresses own intentions, desires, demands, and actions that ought to be reflected, directly or indirectly, by other members of a social network. The active agent in a territory projecting outside is referred to as "I."

A degree of the direct[140] influence on behaviour of various territories is determined by the degree of one's own resolve to hold onto those territories and/or by one's own predispositions of a physiological and psycho-physiological nature. Therefore, the first step

[139]For example, when everybody around starts running in some direction, an impulse to start running in the same direction is quite pronounced.

[140]that is, bypassing conscious consideration

towards dissolution of the territories is to retract the resolve to hold onto them. The second is to bring physiological and psycho-physiological conditions to a roughly neutral position by leading a balanced lifestyle, like that of the Middle Way.

An important example of a territory, projecting inside, is intentions and disposition of a dominant male/female or of a group leader (accepted on a personal level as such). A penetrating shock of displeasure from a dominant male/female is one of the strongest and rarely brought fully to consciousness traumatic experiences of the early years of life. An important example of a territory, projecting outside, is a social position of a group leader, or of an authority.

An excessive emphasis on expanding territories, projecting outside, is a power trip towards the dominant position. An excessive emphasis on expanding territories, projecting inside, is a humility trip towards self-abjection. The path of tantra is to make both projections irrelevant to one's self in order to transcend them. The transcendence leads to dissolution of a big part of that very "self."

In order to attain liberation, all mirrors should be clear[141] and there should be no territories that are stable beyond conscious effort to maintain them.

When a territory, projecting outside, overlaps with a territory, projecting inside, it creates a strong internal conflict, having pronounced psycho-physiological effects (like headache, insomnia, restlessness, etc.). There are two major pathways to react to the conflict: one is to tolerate it and thus "let it unfold," the other is to shift the boundaries[142] of the territories. Behind the choice to shift the boundaries is an urge for definiteness in internal representations of social networks — and it should be resisted. A distinct feature of this pathway is that an adjustment of internal representations of one's own territories happens prior to significant changes in the external circumstances of the conflict, and then an effort is applied to make external circumstances conform to the adopted internal representation. One should strive to form a tolerance to this type of internal conflicts sufficient for the analysis and restructuring of attachments and aversions related to them. To develop this tolerance, one has to observe the avoidance of such internal conflicts and make an effort to keep attention on a conflict, while subjecting it to analysis and deconstruction. It is the resolution of an internal

[141] non-inhibited

[142] The shift of boundaries is reflected as a combination of submissive and aggressive postures.

conflict, prior to attaining a rational view of it, that is the most lasting negative effect of the conflict.

Each territory might be protected from changes by the five armors (see the entry for *kañcuka*).
For a territory, projecting outside,

kalā-tattva is expressed as speech, especially first person, emotionally charged utterances; as face expressions; as assertive body postures;

vidyā-tattva is expressed as wishful thinking (as opposed to seeing things as they are); as pursuit of skills, seen as allowing to control other people; as valuing knowledge only if it is seen as furthering expansion or stability of one's own territories; as the belief that having influence in social networks is necessary for survival;

rāga-tattva is expressed as a bias to see contentment/misery coming primarily from social interactions; as taking interest primarily in social interactions; as an urge "to change the world," or as a desire "to make a difference";

kāla-tattva is expressed as setting the duration, the pace, and the intensity of one's own efforts to maintain/expand a territory;

niyati-tattva is expressed as a belief that influence of "self" on "the external world" should be maintained/expanded; as an idea that projection outside is necessary to counter-balance projections inside; as a sense that life has fixed purpose or meaning;[143] as a belief that loss of all outside projecting territories is death.

For a territory, projecting inside,

kalā-tattva is expressed as a bias towards interpreting any speech as expressing opinions about self; as serving others; as the feeling of guilt; as a reactive behaviour; as transfer of expectations, and of the search for direction outside when inner resources seem exhausted;

vidyā-tattva is expressed as the belief that the social environment is the primary source of knowledge; as having the desire for further differentiation of, and for establishing order in, a social hierarchy as the primary motive for knowledge acquisition; as deriving ideas of one's own influence on others from influences of others upon one's self; as having opinions of others as the basis of self-knowledge;[144]

---

[143] "Man's nature, his spirit, has no set purpose..." – Heraclitus

[144] Since others tend to present their opinions as important, this becomes a self-sustaining illusion.

rāga-tattva is expressed as taking praise and scorn as very relevant and personally important; as connecting praise with having the world more interesting, varied, and colorful; as an inclination to take the advice of fear in the apparent absence of other alternatives;[145]

kāla-tattva is expressed as a modulation of the degree of expression of others' mirrors (for example, blanking out sharp words said by someone close); as set time limits for having certain mirrors active (for example, as deciding to attribute priority to parents' opinions until the age of 13);

niyati-tattva is expressed as casting events in terms that create the illusion of no personal choice involved in the unfolding of events; as seeing an inclusion into social networks as a necessity; as taking opinions, wishes, and intentions of others as imperatives; as acting to fulfill a prophecy.

The above list of *kañcuka* expressions is by no means exhaustive. The real task is to find particular armors of particular territories and then to dissolve them.

Any relaxation of the strength of both types of projections should be done in synch to avoid strong disbalances, for ordinarily both types are finely balanced. Thus, several territories should be made fluid in parallel. For example, removal of modulation of stimulation, reflecting intentions and emotions of others, needs simultaneous dissolution of the transfer of the energy of those intentions or emotions into an imperative, by means of an inside-projecting territory. Such dissolution, in turn, requires a dissolution of outside-projecting territories, used to assert the concept of "I" as a counter balance to projections inside; etc. Successful deconstruction of territories requires opening of energy flows through *chakra-s*, which in turn requires making some territories "fluid."

The key to dissolution of territories is to trace their formation and stability to expressions of one's own will and to psychophysiological mechanisms that protect the psyche from damage. Then, all armors can be dissolved by retraction of resolve-forming expressions of free will. Since dissolution of territories is usually accompanied by quite negative emotions, at such times one has to regulate flows of *prāṇa* and *apāna* to be unobstructed, but ignore the negative reaction in other respects.

[145]Fear gains strong influence over behaviour only when one decides that following fear's advice is good. If this decision is augmented by *rāga-tattva*, then an addiction to fear is developed.

Speech is an instrument of defining "self" in terms of social interactions. The impluse to speak, or to utter words, is, in large part, provided by motives related to positioning in social hierarchies and networks. One consequence of this connection of speech to social networks is that the analysis of inner experiences, memories, intentions, etc. should be on the non-verbal level of raw iconic representation of feelings, memories, and inner gestures, since any expression in language conforms them to views and concepts defined by a social network, the purpose of which is to make the network function smoothly, not to promote liberation.

"I," when uttered or implied by me, is projecting "self" into the space of mirrors to maintain the persistence of "self." This is an effect of *kalā-tattva.* "You," when uttered, or implied, by someone else in reference to me, projects into "inside" territory as an imperative. The sense that it is the best escape from frustration makes a reflected opinion or wish or command such an imperative. This is an effect of *vidyā-tattva.* Both projections are beneficial under certain conditions, especially those of learning and growing up.

The power that social networks exercise over psyche is so great that various traditions sought to use it for attaining liberation. A social group that creates an environment for transcending social hierarchies, including the group itself, is quite conducive to the pursuit of enlightenment. Upaddha Sutta, SN 45.2, makes exactly this point:[146]

> As he was seated to one side, Venerable Ananda said to the Blessed One,[147] "This is half of the holy life, lord: having admirable people as friends, companions and colleagues."
>
> "Don't say that, Ananda. Don't say that. Having admirable people as friends, companions and colleagues is actually the whole of the holy life. When a monk has admirable people as friends, companions, and colleagues, he can be expected to develop and pursue the Noble Eightfold Path."

With the great potential benefits of a group whose members are devoted to the attainment of liberation comes a great danger: that of substituting the quest for enlightenment with the quest for becoming "empowered among the chosen."

[146]Translated from the Pali by Thanissaro Bhikkhu.
[147]Gautama Buddha

The concepts of territory and of mirror significantly contribute to the personal meaning of many important notions.

Death. The personal meaning of one's own death is something that ordinarily is not derived from one's own direct experience of it. The core meaning is derived through analogy with personal impression of the death of another. A living person has corresponding mirrors and territories that are inherently subject to unpredictable change at any moment. Death makes the same mirrors and territories static and subject to collapse, since they no longer possess any resistance or unpredictability. The realization that one's own death would result in a similar vulnerability of one's own mirrors and territories in others connects the idea of death with all negative emotions related to a collapse of one's own territories. "To die" gets the meaning "to let go of all attachments."[148] The lack of expressions of territories, corresponding to referent groups, dissolves the fear of death. Instead of the above meaning, "death" ultimately should be conceptualized as "the end of the infinitely flexible indeterminacy that is the mark of life."

Time. Personal sense of time is created in part by moments of discontinuity in flows of the energy of free will into various territories. By consciously directing these flows into representations of territories that once had active flows, one can evoke *deja vu* experiences. If there are no discontinuities in the flows, sense of time disappears. A discontinuity is created by a *vikalpa*.

Self-confidence. It is developed in the process of acting without reference to either inside or outside projecting territories, but with awareness of mirrors, corresponding to experts in the field.

[148]This might explain why some rites of passage are thought of as a second birth with a new name.

Appendix B.

Mentally painful sensations.

> Be islands unto yourselves,
> refuges unto yourselves,
> seeking no external
> refuge...
>
> *Mahaparinibbana Sutta*

Ordinarily, the only trace a sensation or a feeling leaves is a memory. Some sensations or feelings (for example, estrangement, dejection, shame, scorn, humiliation, anguish, etc.) have more far reaching impact. This happens when a mentally painful sensation has the characteristic of a trauma, due to its intensity or focus.

When sensation reaches the level of trauma, the pursuit of the inhibition of such sensation is an autonomic reaction. The apparent success of this reaction at attaining relief triggers conscious invocation of the inhibition in the future, when the memory of the traumatic experience is about to be recalled. Deeming such invocation as a positive action, it is incorporated into the Ego. The conscious defense of this part of the Ego leads to a philosophical position that values homeostasis. This, in turn, makes invocation of inhibition a generalized strategy that escapes deconstruction through analysis of particular situations where the effect of inhibition turned out to be quite negative.

In order to diminish the influence of this generalized strategy, it should be understood as generalized beyond the area of origin and criticized from positions that make evident the indirect and long-term consequences of gaining short-term relief through the mechanism of inhibition. Therefore, one needs to adhere to a philosophical system that makes clear major consequences of this sort. Total and complete awareness is to be preferred to the comforts of inhibition. The value of the awareness should be established in the philosophical system in order to withstand the tides and storms of emotions. The process of deconstruction of complexes, coagulated around painful sensation, involves pursuing the removal of the causes of the sensation without losing the awareness of the current intensity of the pain. The degree of inhibition should be no higher than required in order to be able to act and to contemplate.

Sometimes a source of mentally painful sensation is a physical pain. An important point in this case is that the physical pain, that might have been a source of the mental pain, might remain in place at the time of removing the inhibition; but instead of psychological inhibition, physiological mechanism of pain moderation would eventually kick in.

There are three steps for removing recurring psychological inhibition of a mentally painful feeling.

1. Establish a preference of complete and uninterrupted awareness before inhibition of painful sensations, be they physical or mental (that is, coming from thoughts, emotions, feelings, or from physical pain like a wound, toothache, numbness in limbs, etc.). This is done:

a. by relating fault conditions in important activities to the lack of awareness due to the preference of inhibition (for example, such fault conditions might manifest themselves as sporadic blackouts caused by a similarity, sometimes very remote, of an anticipated condition to the one being avoided);

b. by a creative search for advantages to the total awareness from the point of view of valued activities;

c. by questioning the anticipated benefits of the inhibition from philosophical positions (by analyzing how it will result in more discomfort, pain, suffering; for example, as *duḥkha* is a result of ignorance that will originate in the inhibition);

d. by actual preference in action, even if the motive is just curiosity as to what would happen if the inhibition were actually abandoned.

2. Abandon all refuges against the pain that have been taken in the past. The refuge in this context means a wall of inhibition, the purpose of which is the un-awareness of mentally painful sensation. Among refuges are

refuge in a person;

refuge in a social hierarchy;

refuge in an intoxicating substance;

refuge in a repetitive, mostly predictable and absorbing activity;

refuge in luck.

Taking refuge results in a least temporary curtailment of awareness, since refuge adds layers of indirection to all interpretations. In general, however, a refuge is a source of ignorance. To abandon a refuge,

a. recollect, in as many "personal feel" details as possible, moments when the refuge was taken;

b. recollect the pain, the inhibition of which was the motive for taking the refuge — its arising, blossoming and waning;

c. recollect the urge to act that leads to the taking of the refuge;

d. recollect the moment when the decision to take the refuge was made;

e. analyze long-term consequences and sacrifices that the taking of the refuge caused;

f. find alternative behaviours that are too specific to become a new refuge;

g. ask yourself, which one of these is worse, given the long-term consequences, and resolve to adopt alternatives;[149]

h. upon the resolve, relive the arising and the blossoming of the pain, and the emergence of the decision to take the refuge. Realize that the decision was just an exercise of your own free will, though poorly informed, and it might be withdrawn the same way it was made. Dissolve the decision by relaxation of intention into meditative awareness.

Abandoning a refuge is very likely to result in quite unpleasant physiological reactions, like disphoria, panic attack, cold sweats, etc. These reactions should be treated with *prāṇāyāma* and the practice of *tattvaśuddhi*, but otherwise ignored and never acted upon.

3. Regulating flows of *prāṇa* and *apāna*, especially through *maṇipūra* and *svādhiṣṭhāna cakra*-s, to support psycho-physiological toleration of the pain.

The rambling of time and *anugraha* take care of the rest.

ॐ

[149]It is better if there is more than one alternative, so that none of them will be dominant.

Appendix C

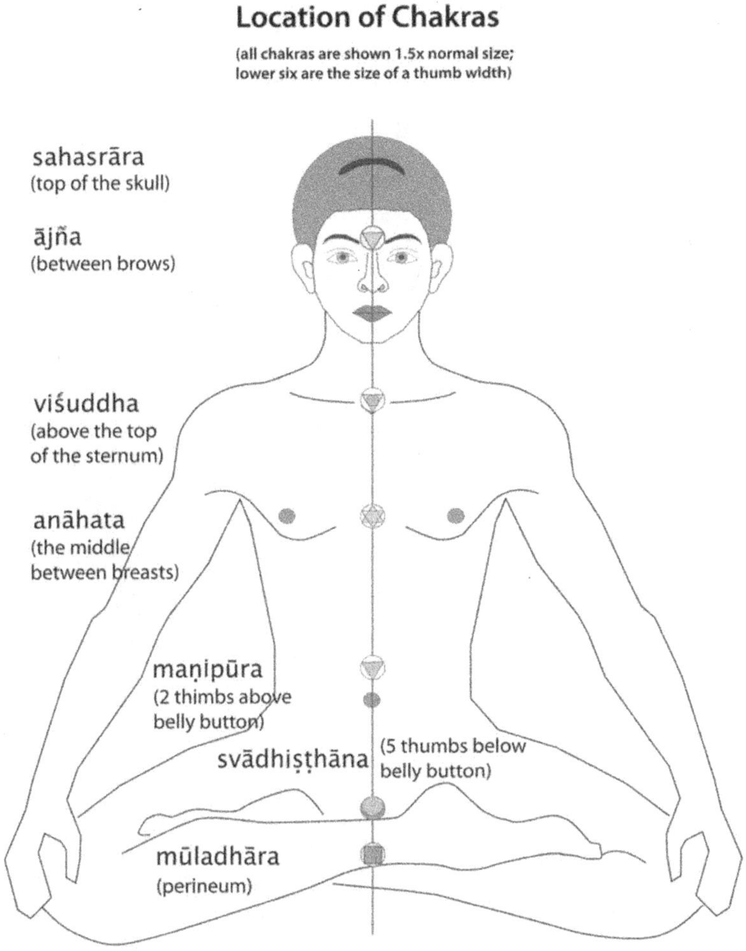
Location of Chakras
(all chakras are shown 1.5x normal size; lower six are the size of a thumb width)
sahasrāra
(top of the skull)
ājña
(between brows)
viśuddha
(above the top of the sternum)
anāhata
(the middle between breasts)
maṇipūra
(2 thimbs above belly button)
svādhiṣṭhāna
(5 thumbs below belly button)
mūladhāra
(perineum)

Bibliography

[Dev87] Swami Vishnu Devananda. *Hatha Yoga Pradipika, The Practical Commentary*. OM Lotus Publications, 1987.

[Iye99] B.K.S. Iyengar. *Light on Pranayama*. The Crossroad Publishing Company, 1999.

[Ram82] Swami Rama. *Enlightment without God*. The Himalayan International Institute of Yoga Science and Philosophy of thew U.S.A., 1982.

[Ram96] Swami Rama. *Path of Fire and Light Vol.2*. The Himalayan Institute Press, 1996.

[Ram98] Swami Rama. *Meditation and Its Practice*. The Himalayan Institute Press, 1998.

[Ram99] Swami Rama. *Living with the Himalayan Masters*. The Himalayan Institute Press, 1999.

[SR98] Alan Hymes Swami Rama, Rudolph Ballentine. *Science of Breath*. The Himalayan Institute Press, 1998.

Index

ego, 54, 60, 67
enlightenment, 2, 77, 83

Trika, 10

ājña, 62
ānandaśakti, **32**, 67
āṇavamala, **46**, 47, 51, 72
āsana, 3, 14, 23
ātman, **13**
ahaṃkāra, **28**, 29, 49
ahaṃkāratattva, **42**, 72
anāhata, 62
anatta (P), 72
antaḥkaraṇa, **29**
antaḥkaraṇa, 43, 48, 72
aṇu, **18**
anugraha, **76**, 78, 87
apāna, 3, **13**, 17, 22, 23, 35, 41
aparāśakti, **32**
avijjā (P), 67, **70**
bhairava, **31**, 32
bhakti, **3**
bhava (P), **72**, 73
buddhi, **25**, 29, 37, 49, 62
buddhīndriya, **43**, 48
buddhitattva, **41**, 42
cakra, **15**
camatkāra, **30**, 67
cit, **30**
citi, **30**, 54, 56, 59, 60, 63, 80–82
cicchakti, **32**
citta, **45**, 63, 66, 67, 71, 80
devadatta, **13**
devatā, **15**
dhāraṇa, 21, **28**, 81
dhanañjaya, **13**
dhyāna, 21, **49**, 50, 51
grāhaka, 57
grāhaka, **11**, 58
grāhya, 57
grāhya, **11**, 58
guṇa, **18**, 24, 28, 29
icchāśakti, 18, **32**, 46, 47, 72
iḍā, 15, 50, 84
īśvaratattva, **35**, 72
jāti (P), **72**, 75
jñānaśakti, 18, **32**, 48
jñāna, **11**
jñānendriya, **42**, 70, 71
jñeya, **11**
kālatattva, **39**, 40, 92
kārmamala, **46**, 47, 48
kalā, 39
kalātattva, **37**, 40, 92
kañcuka, **36**, **40**, 65, 69, 70, 92, 93
karma, **15**, 37, 76
karmendriya, **42**, 48, 70
kriyāśakti, 18, **32**, 48
kṛkala, **13**
kūrma, **13**
māna, **12**, 13
mātṛ, **11**, 65
māyā, **36**, 63, 64, 66, 67
māyāśakti, **36**, 46

māyātattva, **36**, 70
māyīyamala, **46**, 47, 48
mahābhūta, 24, **43**, 44, 70, 71
mala, 24, **46**, 68, 75
manas, **29**, 42, 49, 50
manastattva, **42**, 71
mantra, **51**
mati, **13**, 20, 21, 42
meya, **13**, 81
mūladhāra, 50
nāḍī, 15, **15**
nāga, **13**
nāmarūpa (P), **71**
nimitta, **51**
niyatitattva, **39**, 40, 92
parāparāśakti, 31, **32**
parāśakti, **31, 32**
phassa (P), 71, **71**
piṅgalā, 15, 50, 84
prāṇa, 3, 13, **14**, 17, 22, 23, 35, 41, 50
prāṇāyāma, 14, 23
prājña, **61**, 62
prakāśa, **10**, 11, 12, 17, 18, 30, 32, 42
prakṛti, **24**, 29, 71
prakṛtitattva, **41**, 71
pramāna, **13**
pramātṛ, 12, **12**, 13, 37, 58, 64, 67, 68, 71, 75, 81
prameya, **11**, 12, 13
pratiloma, 72
Pratyabhijñā
  context, vii
  methods, 3
  practices, 2
  subject of, 1
Pratyabhijñāhṛdayam
  context, vii
  text, 8
puruṣa, **24**, 71
puruṣatattva, **41**, 70, 71
puryaṣṭaka, **43**
rāgatattva, **38**, 40, 47, 92
rajas, **18**, 24, 28, 29, 41, 42
sādhana, **2**, 5, 6
sadāśivatattva, **35**
śakti, **30**, 31, 59, 63, 66, 75, 79
śaktitattva, **35**
salāyatana (P), 71, **71**
samādhi, 2, 14, 50, **50**, 51, 65, 85, 87
samāna, **13**
saṃhāra, **76**, 78
saṃjñā, **13**, 58
saṃsāra, 32, **46**, 72, 73, 75, 76
saṃsārin, **46**, 75, 76, 79
saṃskāra, **45**, 70, 76
saṃvid, **17**
saṅkhārā (P), 70
śarīra, **45**
sattarka, **3**
sattva, **18**, 24, 28, 29, 41, 42
śiva, 18, **30**, 31, 32
śivatattva, **34**
skandha, **45**
sṛṣṭi, **76**, 78
sthiti, 71, **76**, 78
śuddhavidyātattva, **35**, 71
suṣumnā, 14, 15, 84
svātantrya, **29**, 30
taijasa, **61**, 62
tamas, **18**, 24, 28, 29, 41, 42
taṇhā (P), **71**, 73
tanmātra, **43**, 70, 71
tattva, **32**, 33, 63, 69, 70
tirodhāna, 72, **76**, 78, 82
turīya, **61**
udāna, **13**
upādāna (P), **71**, 72, 73
vāyu, **13**, 22, 50
vairagya, **22**, 24, 73
vaiśvānara, **61**, 62
vedanā (P), **71**, 73

vidyātattva, **37**, 40, 70, 92
vijñāna, 70
vikalpa, 7, **21**
vimarśa, **29**, 30, 46, 57
viññāṇa (P), **70**, 71, 73
visargaḥ
  śāṃbhavaḥ, 67
  śāktaḥ, 67
  āṇavaḥ, 67
viśuddha, 50, 62
viśva, **13**
vyāna, **13**
vyutthāna, **50**, 87
yoga, **2**

www.ingramcontent.com/pod-product-compliance
Lightning Source LLC
Chambersburg PA
CBHW022028090426
42739CB00006BA/333
* 9 7 8 0 6 1 5 2 6 2 6 8 0 *